FIRST

FIRST

WHAT IT TAKES TO WIN

TYNDALE HOUSE PUBLISHERS, INC., CAROL STREAM, ILLINOIS

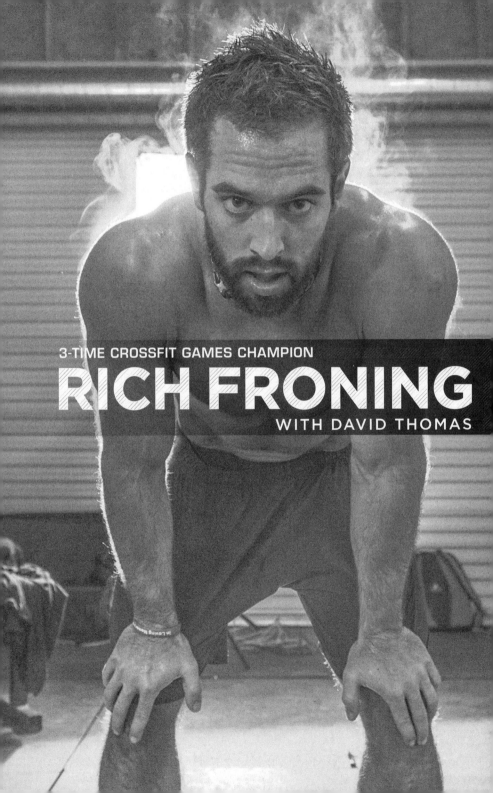

3-TIME CROSSFIT GAMES CHAMPION

RICH FRONING

WITH DAVID THOMAS

Visit Tyndale online at www.tyndale.com.

TYNDALE and Tyndale's quill logo are registered trademarks of Tyndale House Publishers, Inc.

First: What It Takes to Win

Designed by Alberto C. Navata Jr.

Edited by Jeremy Taylor

Library of Congress Cataloging-in-Publication Data

Froning, Rich.
  First : what it takes to win / Rich Froning and David Thomas.
    pages cm
  Includes index.
  ISBN 978-1-4143-8678-2 (sc)
  1. Froning, Rich. 2. Athletes—United States—Biography. 3. CrossFit Games. I. Title.
  GV697.F76A3 2013
  796.092—dc23
  [B]   2013011720

Printed in the United States of America

19   18   17   16   15
8   7

To Donnie (DGH) and Matt (MJH) Hunsucker . . .
I miss you guys every day.

To Meme (JCF) . . . for all the things you
taught me and still teach me every day.

To Grandpa Finn . . . Even though I never really got to know you,
you are the man behind an incredible and supportive family.

CONTENTS

FOREWORD

RICH FRONING IS the most powerful CrossFit athlete I know.

Our sport tests for the fittest person alive, and we do this by evaluating power output across varying time domains with a variety of functional movements—from short-duration efforts with really heavy weight to long-duration efforts with light or no weight. Consistently having faster times in completing these tasks equates to being fitter and more powerful. At the end of a CrossFit Games competition, we have tested fairly for the fittest alive, and in these tests Rich has been dominant.

In 2010 Rich won his Sectional and Regional competitions before going on to take second at the CrossFit Games. In 2011 he placed third in the first-ever CrossFit Open and followed that up with his first CrossFit Games victory.

In 2012 he accomplished what I think is one of the most impressive feats in the seven-year existence of our sport. Rich started the 2012 season by winning the five-week Open, in which athletes were given five days to complete a workout that was released each Wednesday. Competing against thousands of athletes from around the world, Rich took first in two events and was in the top three in two of the others.

Rich then advanced to the Central East Regional and won the event. The Regionals differ from the Open in that you have six workouts to do over the course of three days. The events are announced well ahead of time, and the competition includes a handful of other elite CrossFit athletes. Top finishers earn spots in the CrossFit Games.

To round out the 2012 season, Rich won the CrossFit Games for a second straight year. The Games differ from the Open and the Regionals in that athletes compete in unknown and unknowable challenges. Most events are not announced until shortly before the competition—sometimes just minutes before. Just as in 2011, Rich won the Games in dominant fashion after building up an early lead that was too difficult for anyone to overcome.

He is the first and only two-time male CrossFit Games champion, and in three Games appearances he has never finished below second.

The hat trick of winning the Open, the Regional, and the Games in 2012 will be hard to replicate by anyone else as the sport grows, and Rich might be the only person capable of doing it again.

These accomplishments aside, Rich's power transcends his physical strength and tremendous work capacity.

The first time I met Rich, I was impressed with how humble and gracious he was. He had just won the 2010

Southeast Regional, and he was smiling and shaking hands with people. I could tell he genuinely cared about those around him. When you spoke to him, he listened to you as if nothing was more important than what you had to say. He was young but already a great representative of the sport.

Over the past few years, the sport has grown quickly, and I've watched Rich grow as an integral part of it. The Rich I met in 2010 has not changed with his fame. He still smiles and shakes hands with those who want to meet him. He still genuinely cares about those around him. And when you speak, he still listens to you as if there is nothing more important than what you are talking about.

The next few years are going to bring more growth for the sport and more fame for Rich. He is a star, and his star is going to shine brighter and brighter.

But Rich will stay the same: true to himself, true to his fans, true to his family, and true to his faith.

Rich Froning is the most powerful CrossFit athlete I know.

Dave Castro
Director, CrossFit Games, CrossFit Training

PROLOGUE

FIVE FEET.

That was all I needed to reach the top of the rope.

Five feet had never looked so far away.

I was fifteen feet above the ground, hanging on for dear life to a rope dangling from a massive steel structure. My grip was shot, and I could hardly even hear the hundreds of screaming spectators in the Home Depot Center in Carson, California. I was hot, drenched in sweat, and utterly exhausted.

I released my left hand to grab the rope above my right. Almost six minutes into attempting to conquer this stinking twenty-foot rope climb, I was absolutely determined to make it to the top. But in the final event of the 2010 CrossFit Games, after three days of being run through a physical and mental wringer like nothing I had ever experienced, it was all I could do to get my left hand up and onto the rope.

I began kicking my legs, looking for every possible bit of momentum to help me make it to the top. By this point I was so far behind the competition, I knew I wouldn't come close to finishing the workout before the twelve-minute time cap. But there was no way I was going to fail on this attempt. I had already failed more times than I could count.

When I finally reached the top and stretched my left hand up to touch the bar the rope was hanging from, there was no time for celebration. I could tell right away that my right hand wasn't going to be able to hold up my weight on its own.

I put my left hand back on the rope, below my right one, but the downward slide had begun, and my arms and shoulders were too taxed to stop it. The friction from the rope ripped into my palms and fingers. My burning hands reacted by doing what made sense to them: they let go.

The landing twenty feet below was abrupt and awkward. My pride hit the ground first. Then my heels, and the momentum of the fall rocked me backward. My butt was next to make contact with the ground. The back of my head and neck struck an orange bucket of chalk next to the rig.

Physically and mentally spent, I didn't even feel the landing. It wasn't until later that I learned just how hard I had fallen.

And it wasn't until the event was finished that I learned just what the rope failure had cost me: the CrossFit Games championship and title of Fittest Man on Earth.

It would have made for a great story, a complete unknown from small-town Tennessee coming out of nowhere to defeat the greatest CrossFit athletes in the world.

But then, the rope.

Two years and two Games championships later, I still get asked by those in the CrossFit community about that rope and how it cost me the title. They suggest that if it hadn't been for the rope, I would be a *three*-time Games champion.

But the truth is, if not for that rope, I don't think I would be a three-time champ. Or even a two-time champion. I am convinced I would not have won another Games.

There is something those people don't know about the rope. Or me.

The rope changed my life.

CHAPTER I

"JUST WORK"

THIS IS JUST WORK!

The final event on the second day of the 2010 CrossFit Games was called the Sandbag Move. My assigned judge began describing the details of the event as I walked out onto the stadium floor toward an empty wheelbarrow that was waiting for me.

We would have to throw 600 pounds of sandbags from the seats at one end of the stadium onto the ground, load them into a wheelbarrow, haul them across the stadium, and then carry the bags up the steps to the top row at that end of the stadium.

The description just as easily could have been coming

from my dad, assigning me yet another of the many random chores he gave me when I was growing up to instill within me a strong work ethic.

I knew the Sandbag Move had to be catching some of the other competitors off guard. But to me, it seemed like just another day of getting work done back home in Tennessee.

The Sandbag Move is a classic example of how random the events at the Games are. And, at least at times, how practical they can be.

At its core, CrossFit consists of real-world movements that people use every day, throughout the day: picking things up, carrying them, lifting them overhead, pulling them, pushing them, dragging them.

Granted, for most people, hauling sandbags in a wheelbarrow across a sports stadium isn't an everyday activity itself. The Sandbag Move is one of those Games events that can make you scratch your head and ask, "Where on earth did this idea come from? Who thought it up? And how bad of a mood was he in when he thought of it?" But that's what the Games are—facing the challenges delivered by the unknown and the unknowable.

We had twenty minutes to complete the workout, and I finished in seven minutes, fourteen seconds—good enough to win my heat of six competitors and finish second among the twenty-four who had advanced to that point in the Games. My second-place finish moved me into first place overall, heading into the third and final day.

When I caught up with my family and friends after

completing the Sandbag Move, my dad's first words to me were "You're welcome."

I must admit, my dad had prepared me well, because as I grew up, long before the CrossFit Games had been created, he made sure I stayed busy doing the unknown and the unknowable.

Odd Jobs

Most of the time around our place when I was growing up, there was some chore or other to be done. And when there wasn't, one could easily be created.

Like most kids I knew, I played video games, but my gaming systems were never the coolest ones to have. So I spent a lot of time outside, playing sports and games or finding outdoorsy activities to do in the woods where we lived. Besides, if I didn't find anything to do outside, my parents would come up with something that would get me out of the house. I could either find an outdoor game or activity that I wanted to do, or I could spend the rest of the time until sundown performing a chore I didn't want to do.

There were plenty of times when the jobs my parents thought up for me made no sense. Like the summer when Dad pointed to a pile of old lumber filled with rusty nails.

"I'm gonna use those boards," he told me, "so I need you to pull all those nails out."

I'm sure I looked at him kind of funny, because the assignment seemed odd.

"Besides," he added, "pulling those nails will help you with throwing a curveball."

A kid dreaming of a major-league baseball career, I actually believed that and did as ordered, pulling every single nail out of every one of those boards. Then the wood just sat there, unused, for a couple of weeks until Dad finally threw it onto a pile with a bunch of other junk and lit a bonfire.

Come on, I thought, remembering how Dad had said he had plans for using the wood.

There was another time when I had made Dad a little angry, although I can't recall what stupid act I had committed.

We had two barns on our property about fifty yards apart, and inside one was a big pile of cinder blocks. Dad told me to take the cinder blocks from that barn and move them into the other barn and stack them there. It took me about three hours to complete the task, carrying two blocks at a time, and when I finished, I was actually rather proud of how neatly I had stacked them. I mean, they had been just tossed into a pile in the other barn.

When Dad came home from his job, he examined my work.

"You know what?" he said. "I don't like where those are at. Why don't you move that pile back over to the other barn."

I had to spend the next three hours moving all those cinder blocks back to where they had been in the first place. Except I had to stack them neatly instead of throwing them into a pile.

At least that time I had the assignment coming for getting into trouble.

I learned early that when possible, it was best to make work fun.

One job I always had in the fall was to pile up apples that had fallen from the trees in our yard and haul them off so they wouldn't rot on the ground and attract bees. I turned apple picking into a baseball game, taking a Wiffle ball bat and imagining I was Cecil Fielder from the Detroit Tigers, launching majestic home runs over the power lines and into the seats of Tiger Stadium. In reality, when belting baseballs rather than apples, I was a line-drive hitter more along the lines of my favorite player, shortstop Alan Trammell. But what does it hurt for a kid to pretend?

Work and Play

Both my parents believed in hard work. Raised to have a strong work ethic, they were intent on passing that trait down to their children.

I was the only boy, so the hardest work landed on me. My sister, Kayla, is four-and-a-half years younger than I am. We're complete opposites. I think she might have played one year of T-ball growing up, but other than that, the closest she wanted to get to sports was as a cheerleader.

Kayla was diagnosed with type 1 diabetes when she was twelve, and after that, I teased her about taking advantage of the diabetes to massage the system and get off the hook for a lot of the work.

There was no getting out of work for me, though.

I did my fair share of grumbling and complaining under my breath, but I noticed that my parents both modeled hard work. They weren't sitting on the couch and telling me to go do something; they were working hard too.

My dad always had a project—or three—going at home. Dad, who now is head of maintenance with the Oreck vacuum cleaner company, was skilled with his hands and always building, making, or fixing something. Mom worked as a waitress, and when she wasn't doing that job, she seemed to be constantly cleaning either our house or someone else's. Both inside and outside, it seemed my parents always had something they were working on at home. I could count on one hand all the times I remember seeing my parents lounging around doing nothing.

My parents were both products of families that believed hard work will get you where you need to go. I grew up hearing my parents, grandparents, and aunts and uncles telling my cousins and me that working hard would bring us advantages later in life. We were taught that everything we would need as we grew older wouldn't just be handed to us; we would have to work for much of it.

My dad, Rich Sr., was raised in a home where his father was dedicated to his job: my grandpa worked at General Motors for forty years. My mom, Janice, grew up on a parsnip and turnip farm. She had eight brothers and sisters, and being a farming family, they had projects year-round they needed to work on together.

Their families were mostly from north of Detroit,

Michigan, and we lived in that area, near the small town of Romeo, until I was almost five. Then a job transfer for my dad took us to Cookeville, Tennessee, where I still live.

The transfer took place under somewhat unusual circumstances. Dad worked at TRW Automotive and was operating a machine that packed air bag reactors with sodium azide, a highly flammable and potentially explosive dust. Apparently the room in the plant where all the excess dust was sucked up and collected hadn't been cleaned as it should have been. Dad was tightening a screw on the machine during the workers' lunch break, and the screw grew hot and ignited the dust. The dust went up into the vent and into the room that hadn't been cleaned, and that caused an explosion. No one was injured, but Dad said he was within an arm's length of having a cinder block wall fall on him.

The explosion was not Dad's fault, and out of everything that happened with the accident, he wound up being promoted to maintenance supervisor and transferred to TRW's plant in Cookeville, which is about halfway between Nashville and Knoxville on Interstate 40. We laughed about Dad's blowing up a plant being his path to a job promotion.

My parents purchased a home on five acres outside of Cookeville. We also owned five acres across the street, and with that much land, there was always some type of work to do.

After coming home from work at the plant, Dad would get busy working around our house. I didn't think there was anything on a car he couldn't fix or anything he couldn't build out of wood. He enjoyed showing me how to build or fix things. That was our time to be together, just the two of us guys, and we both treasured it. At the end of the day or when the job was completed, I was the designated cleanup boy. Because I liked to work out, Dad would find ways to turn my chores into workouts. The benefits to my baseball career seemed to be his go-to reason whenever I balked.

Mom and Dad not only kept me busy, but they also had no hesitation coming up with work for my friends to do. Friends who would come over to see me mostly lived in subdivisions and weren't used to having to do the type of chores I did. That didn't stop my parents from trying to "help them out" by putting them to work.

After my friends left, I would tell my parents that my friends were threatening to stop coming over to see me because of the work they were made to do. But my parents thought everybody would benefit from knowing how to work hard.

I couldn't escape chores even when we returned to Michigan to visit family. One of my aunts would put my cousins and me to work just like my dad did. Uncle Don and Aunt Chris had five acres, and Aunt Chris would have us rake grass clippings from the mowing because she believed that the clippings would kill the grass. Five acres of grass clippings is a lot.

Aunt Chris also frequently told us to go to a field that had been recently plowed and pick up big rocks and haul them back to put around the perimeter of the large pond on their property. Even now when I see that pond, with rocks all the way around it, I think back to how much work it took for us to make the pond look nice.

Now that I'm older, I'm thankful for the work ethic my parents and family cultivated in me. Not only has it paid off for me in CrossFit competitions, but I can look back to when I played high school baseball and later when I worked as a fireman and developed a reputation for being a hard worker. It's true what I heard from my extended family growing up: people who work hard gain an advantage over those who don't.

CHAPTER 2

GROWING UP A FRONING

THE WORST PART about our move to Tennessee was being taken away from our family in Michigan, and it was a lot of family. Just on my mom's side alone, I have thirty-two first cousins. Twenty-five of us are boys.

My competitive nature derives from having that many cousins, because when we visited Michigan or when I spent parts of my summers there with them, competitions inevitably broke out. It could have been sports, video games, paintball, hunting, whatever. You name it, and we found a way to turn it into a competition.

One of our favorite games was King of the Dock. In the middle of Uncle Don and Aunt Chris's pond—the one with the pretty rocks around it—was a wooden platform that we would swim out to and play an aquatic version of King of the Hill. As the number of participating cousins climbed, so did the difficulty in remaining king—we weren't exactly playing touch football on that dock.

King of the Dock was cutthroat. There were no rules, and it didn't matter if you were ten or twenty years old—whatever methods it took to get you thrown off the dock were fair game. It was common for games to end when a fight broke out. Sometimes not even a fight could halt the games. Or interrupt them.

I wasn't a big kid growing up, but I was the fifth-oldest cousin, so I could hold my own on the dock. But still, anyone who was beginning to establish a lasting presence on the platform would face an onslaught of a hastily put-together alliance of cousins intent on ending his reign. The numbers always won out.

The competitiveness wasn't limited to when we were together. We'd call each other—and later, e-mail and text—to compare our baseball seasons or how fast we had run or how much weight we had lifted, or anything, really, that we could compare.

Our dads would even get into comparing their sons' latest accomplishments, but it was always a healthy competition. We rooted for each other because we took great pride in our family's successes. But while rooting for my cousins to do well, I also wanted to do slightly better than all of them.

The Trailer

My grandparents from my dad's side, John (Papa) and Jeanne (Meme), came down to Tennessee often to visit us. In fact, they wound up buying a mobile home to stay in and put it on our property because my grandmother was the type of person who was concerned that she was somehow getting in our way when they visited. My grandparents typically stayed two or three weeks at a time, and it was great to be able to spend stretches of time like that with them before they had to go back home.

My dad wound up moving into that trailer when he and Mom divorced while I was a sophomore in high school. They had divorced when I was a year old, but they got back together and remarried a couple of years later.

When Mom and Dad divorced the second time, it was hard on my sister. Kayla was eleven, and while I was old enough to understand that the divorce wasn't our fault, she struggled with that.

We stayed with Mom in our house, but the good thing for us was that because of the trailer, our dad was only a hundred yards away. While I was going through high school, my parents got along. All I had to do whenever I wanted to see Dad was walk to his trailer, and I was able to sleep in my same bed without having to go back and forth between my parents.

Family of Faith

My mom, Grandma Meme, and my other grandmother, Violet, had the greatest spiritual influence on me growing up. All of

Mom's family was Catholic, and they were *devout* Catholics. They didn't miss a Sunday mass. On my dad's side, my grandpa was Catholic—he attended Notre Dame, and that made me a lifelong Fighting Irish fan—but my grandmother wasn't.

Papa and Meme were very sincere in their faith, but they didn't attend church together. Meme had attended nondenominational churches until she married Papa; then she went through all the steps to join the Catholic church. But she never really adopted all the Catholic ways and eventually returned to attending a Protestant church. Later on, my grandfather, after retiring from GM, also left the Catholic church for a nondenominational church.

All the years I was growing up, I wondered why Papa and Meme attended different churches but never asked about it. As an adult, I finally had a long talk with my grandfather about his and Meme's spiritual journey, and I learned so much about both of them that I wished we'd had that conversation a long time earlier.

Dad attended mass when I was a kid, but he was such a fidgeter that he had trouble sitting through an entire service and usually left after the homily.

When our family moved to Tennessee, we discovered that Catholic churches weren't nearly as numerous as they were back in Michigan, and we set out to find a new church home.

I remember attending a Presbyterian church for a while before finally settling in at a Baptist church. My impression at the time was that we were a spiritual family. We always read from the Bible the story of Jesus' resurrection at Easter, and at Christmas we read the real Christmas story, not the Santa Claus story.

Our church had a children's pastor, Ms. Julie, whose Sunday services I enjoyed a lot, and partly because of her influence, I asked Jesus into my heart as a sixth grader. Even at that young age, I understood that I was a sinner and that Jesus had died in order to take away the penalty for my wrongdoing. That's the message of the gospel in a nutshell, and I fully believed and embraced it.

Whether we were attending a Catholic, Presbyterian, or Baptist church, prayer was strongly emphasized in our family. I prayed every night, and on nights when I hadn't prayed for whatever reason, I couldn't fall asleep. I'd be lying in bed wondering why I was still awake and I'd realize, *Oh, yeah— I didn't pray!* Then I'd say my nightly prayer and off to sleep I'd soon be.

Looking back, though, I see how shallow my prayers were, even throughout my teenage years. The communication was one-sided because my prayers were selfish—asking God to give me what I wanted or to keep my family safe so something bad wouldn't happen. My prayers were all about me either not hurting or fulfilling my desires.

I also see now that church attendance was almost a duty for me. My mind-set was that because we were Christians, we were supposed to go to church. I wasn't attending church because I wanted to go. I think that's the way my family viewed attending mass when we were in Michigan, and that carried over for me when we moved to Tennessee. It bothers me now that I felt that way, but that's how it was, and there's nothing I can do to go back and change it, as much as I might like to.

The upside of church attendance for me was that I established a little bit of a foundation of Bible knowledge. When I was younger, Meme gave me a children's Bible that was a whole lot easier to read than an adults' Bible. Because of Meme's gift, I knew the main Bible stories. Daniel in the lions' den was my favorite, and I also enjoyed reading about David defeating the giant Goliath in battle. In fact, I liked any story that involved David.

But there wasn't much discussion of the Bible around our house. I guess because my parents were so busy with their jobs and working on their projects, we didn't have any set times when they could explain to my sister and me any of the stories we were reading in our children's Bibles.

The downside of my spiritual journey from my early years, as I've said, was that by the time I entered high school, I was attending church more out of duty than desire. Further, my prayer life consisted of me telling God what I wanted instead of growing in my relationship with Him. As a result, a few years later, I reached a point where, because my relationship with God wasn't as meaningful to me as it should have been, it was easy for my faith to grow dormant.

CHAPTER 3

STARS AND STRIKES

THE MOST IMPORTANT aspects of my life, in this order, are faith, family, and fitness. Faith and family always have been a part of my life. Fitness joined in the summer before my eighth-grade year.

I liked to eat a lot, and going into the eighth grade, I was a little thick. I say "a little thick" because I wasn't pudgy or anything like that. But my cousins were not even a little thick. The movie *300* had not been filmed yet, but the Spartan soldiers in that movie are the best way of describing how my cousins looked compared to me. That made me self-conscious about my body. Determined to change my physique so I would look more like my cousins, I started cutting back on the amount of food I ate.

With football season nearing, I came down with the flu and strep throat in the same week and lost what for an athletic eighth grader amounted to a lot of weight. When I recovered, I was concerned about the shape I was in, so I went and talked with Coach Cook, the strength coach for the football team. Following his advice, I started lifting weights and doing some cardiovascular exercises, and I immediately fell in love with the physical exertion.

My genetics must have been workout friendly, because it didn't take long for me to get myself into good shape. I began to like the way I looked. Working out, and the results I quickly saw, gave me a confidence boost. I was hooked.

I trained five or six days a week, and seven if I could, with my sessions heavy on push-ups, curls, and shoulder presses. I worked out with dumbbells and lifted using an old weight set from Sears that my dad had.

Baseball was my sport, and I planned on making it to the major leagues as a middle infielder. I wasn't comfortable being the center of attention, and I loved baseball because it was a team sport made up of individual components. When I was at the plate, it was me versus the pitcher. It was a one-on-one matchup that gave me the opportunity to measure myself competitively against another individual, yet it came within the context of a team sport environment. I could have my one-on-one games within the game, but in the end, all the focus was on the team's result.

In my seventh- and eighth-grade years, I played basically year-round on a travel team. As a freshman in high school, I began playing for the Cookeville High Cavaliers. At first I loved it, but then we had a new baseball coach come in before my sophomore year, and for some reason the new coach and I didn't really hit it off. I still don't know what the problem was, but he didn't seem to like me.

My sophomore year was a difficult one. That's the year my parents divorced, and because I felt like the new baseball coach didn't like me, I stopped liking baseball. I don't know how much those two situations had to do with one another, but I had previously had such a passion for baseball, and I completely lost it that year.

I had intended to play football as a freshman, but right before preseason practices, I changed my mind. I thought taking time out from baseball to play football might hurt my chances of playing beyond high school. Also, my parents were concerned that I wasn't big enough for football and that I might get injured.

I didn't play football as a sophomore either, but because I didn't want to go through off-season baseball practices with the coach I didn't like, my junior year I decided to go ahead and play football. I was a cornerback and played a little bit of slot receiver. In the third game of the season, I dove to recover an onside kick, and when the pile of players landed on top of me, my right shoulder dislocated. My season ended that night.

Before baseball season my junior year, we changed coaches

again, and while I was glad to learn of the switch, I had no idea how important the new coach would become for me.

Butch Chaffin had played baseball and been a team captain at Cookeville High. He had also played in college and was an assistant coach at the college level for a few years. He's still the baseball coach at Cookeville, and during his career he has coached more than one hundred players who have gone on to play in college. He definitely knows how to develop baseball players, but more than that, he knows how to develop teenagers into young men. Coach Chaffin is an inspirational man who was profoundly influential in my becoming who I am today. I consider him one of my closest friends and most trusted advisers.

My football injury was to my throwing shoulder. I told Coach Chaffin about it, but I hid from him how serious the injury actually was. My shoulder kept dislocating—about ten times that school year. I eventually cracked the humeral head and tore the labrum, and it needed surgery. But I wanted to play college baseball, and the junior season is crucial for being noticed by recruiters and scouts. I didn't want to miss a game that season.

The strategy I adopted was not to warm up by throwing before games, like my teammates all did. Instead, I used a Thera-Band to get my shoulder loose and then made as few throws as possible to get ready for the game. Fortunately I played second base and didn't have to make long throws but could throw sidearm to first to take some of the burden off my shoulder. I played through the pain and made it until after the season before undergoing reconstructive surgery to repair the labrum.

I didn't recognize it at the time, and neither did he, but Coach Chaffin put us through workouts that prepared me well for CrossFit. Running was an integral part of our training; we players used to joke that we ran more than the track team. There also were days when we would spend up to an hour and a half in the weight room. Over the course of a weight-lifting session, we might do five or six hundred sit-ups or three or four hundred push-ups between our various lifts. Coach kept us moving the entire hour and a half.

Coach has since told me that he put us through that grind in part to see how far he could push each of us mentally. He kept emphasizing the need for mental toughness regardless of what would come our way. He told us we couldn't know what would happen to us during a game, but no matter what did take place, our minds had to be prepared to deal with it. Sometimes I thought he was trying to see if he could break us, but I liked the challenge. I really responded to his style of coaching, and I looked up to him because he was interested in us as people and not just baseball players.

I had batted in the leadoff position during my long sophomore season, and Coach Chaffin kept me in that role my junior year. For my senior season, in 2005, he moved me into the three hole. I hit about .400 for my high school career, and although I wasn't a big power hitter, I did have enough power to hit the gaps and be a consistent doubles hitter. I made the all-district team a couple of times and was named all-region.

I was a team captain, but I was more of a lead-by-example captain than a rah-rah-type leader. I was a good player, but I never felt like I was a great player or our best player. In fact, four other seniors off the team my final year at Cookeville played in college.

We had a good team on which the players fit well together. We each had our strengths and weaknesses, but our abilities all complemented each other. We also were a close team. The guys on my baseball team were my best friends, and I'm still close friends with several of them.

We belonged to a tough district. My junior year, we played a memorable game against Blackman High School from Murfreesboro. Blackman's best player was David Price, who became the first overall pick in the 2007 Major League Baseball draft. In 2009 he was a full-time starter for the Tampa Bay Rays, and in 2012 he won the American League Cy Young Award. He's phenomenal now in the majors, and he was a phenom then, too.

On our home field, in an extra-inning game that lasted into the ninth, Price struck out twenty-one of us. He's six foot six now, and he might have been that tall in high school. (He also was an outstanding basketball player at Blackman.) Because of his height, he had a long stride toward home plate. He also hid the ball really well, and his pitches were on you in the blink of an eye. Best I can remember, he struck me out three times that game. I remember for certain, though, that he hit me with a pitch—a fastball—right in the middle of my left thigh. And it didn't feel good. I did what any self-respecting, tough-as-nails baseball player would do: I didn't rub where he hit me. Not until I reached first base, anyway. Then I rubbed it. That hurt!

Not being able to make contact against David Price that day was my most frustrating experience as an athlete until the rope in 2010.

Another frustration was the way that season ended, though I learned a valuable lesson about team dynamics. We were cochampions of our district that year. In Tennessee, after the regular season, the postseason progressed from district tournaments to regional tournaments to the state tournament. Late in the season, we had two or three guys who started bickering with each other, and that damaged the team chemistry that had been perhaps our greatest strength. We didn't even make it out of the district tournament, ending our season earlier than we had expected.

One thing I probably led our team in was dirt on the uniform. I didn't feel like I had as much talent as some of my teammates, so I knew I had to work my butt off to contribute to my team. I had felt that way all the way back when I started playing baseball, and I made up for it by trying to be the dirtiest kid on the field. As an infielder, I dove for just about every ground ball that was remotely within reach. My mom can attest to that from all the stained uniforms she had to wash throughout my playing career.

My sophomore year, on more than one occasion during practices, I dove for ground balls on asphalt. When the field was too wet from rain, we would throw and take grounders on the school parking lot. You'd figure the first set of scrapes would have taught me to save the diving for the dirt infield, but it didn't. I took a lot of ribbing from my teammates about that.

After my junior season, a few junior colleges offered me scholarships, and I chose to attend Walters State Community College in eastern Tennessee. Walters State had a strong baseball program and reached the Junior College World Series the year I graduated from high school. Coach Chaffin had played there and suggested it would be a good place for me to continue my career. Walters State was about a two-and-a-half-hour drive from home, and I figured that would be far enough away without being too far.

I was wrong about that.

I was miserable almost immediately after setting foot on campus. There wasn't one thing I could point to as the problem. That was my first time away from home, so I guess I was homesick. Plus, baseball at the college level felt like a job because it was so serious and intense. And I think Coach Chaffin had spoiled me. That's nothing against the Walters State coaches, because I don't think I would have found a coach anywhere whom I would have liked as much as Coach Chaffin.

In all fairness, I didn't give the coaches there enough time even to see if they cared about me. I was at Walters State just two months before leaving. I didn't last until our first game of the fall season before I dropped out and returned home with no idea what I would do next.

CHAPTER 4

FIGHTING FIRES

DAD KNEW ONE THING I was going to be doing after I returned home: working.

"You've got to have a job if you're going to be home," he told me.

I took a job at the TRW factory where my dad worked, and from six in the morning until four in the afternoon, I helped assemble air bags. That job was one of the worst experiences of my life. I worked on an assembly line, and we would rotate to different tasks during the day. For an hour I would put nuts and bolts on air bags. Then I'd spend another hour putting inflators or reactors into air bags. Then I'd spend another hour sticking the Ford emblem on steering wheels.

I've known people who have held jobs like that for thirty or forty years, and I have tremendous respect for their staying power. My personality was not a good fit for that assembly line. It was the most miserable, most tedious job I could imagine. I stuck it out for six long months.

Working on the assembly line certainly offered me plenty of time to think, and I reached a conclusion: *I'm going back to school.*

Learning on the Job

Cookeville is the home of Tennessee Tech University, and when I looked into taking classes there, I discovered that the school had a student-firefighter program in partnership with the Cookeville Fire Department. I learned that I could attend classes at TTU and pay for them by working full-time with the fire department. I would get paid per call that I went out on.

Because of the timing of when I joined the program, I was unable to go to fire school right away. I had to study my way through a thick binder to answer questions about firefighting, but not having been through fire school, I could not actually go into a fire. I could ride along, but at a fire, I would have to stand and observe alongside Benton Young, the driver and engineer. It was pretty boring to be at a fire and not be able to fight alongside the other firemen.

There was a lieutenant named Marvin Montgomery, and I thought he hated my guts. He would ridicule me and make me feel like an idiot for any little thing I did wrong—and sometimes for things I didn't think I had done wrong. With the one-day-on, two-days-off firefighter's schedule, that meant I had to be around Lieutenant Montgomery for a full twenty-four hours at a time. And it seemed like he was on my back all 86,400 seconds of each shift. I almost quit the fire department and the TTU program because of Lieutenant Montgomery. However, I liked the idea of being a firefighter and not owing money when I graduated from college more than I disliked the mental beat-downs.

It turned out that Lieutenant Montgomery was merely testing me and pushing me mentally, although in a less recognizable manner than Coach Chaffin had. After I'd completed my training, Lieutenant Montgomery told me that he'd had a twofold purpose for the way he treated me. First, he wanted to make sure I learned what I needed to learn to become a firefighter. Second, he needed to see if I could be trusted to do the right thing when I entered a burning building—a scenario that could be potentially deadly not just for me but for the other firefighters as well.

Benton Young found ways to test me too, though his methods were different from the lieutenant's. Partly motivated by not wanting to mess up, I learned what I needed to learn and proved myself to Lieutenant Montgomery and Benton. Their methods might not have presented the most comfortable learning environment for me, but they worked, and through them we developed good friendships that remain in place today.

Close Call and Questions

I went through the eight-week fire-school academy with a group of other student-firefighters in the summer of 2006. After fire school, one of the first big fires I went into was at a two-story house. We had been to that house earlier in the day for a fire in the attic, had put out the flames, and left thinking we had taken care of everything. I'm not sure exactly what happened after we left, but there were suspicions that the fire had been reset for insurance purposes. Regardless, we were called back to the house a couple of hours later.

The house was fully aflame when we arrived. I was second on the nozzle, backing up the guy in front who was spraying the fire. Those hoses are heavy and will get out of control in a hurry if you don't have two firefighters handling them. We entered through the front door and started spraying. Above the roar of the flames, I could hear things falling around us. Then, all of a sudden, part of the ceiling dropped. The lieutenant who had come to the scene grabbed me and tried to pull us both through the door. I don't know how he did it because he wasn't exactly the fittest guy. But he backed out of the door, half-dragging both of us, just before the ceiling caved in right where we had been standing.

You might think that being inside a burning building and having everything suddenly start crashing in around me would have been unnerving. But actually it was kind of cool. That's part of my thrill-seeker personality, I guess.

Being a fireman exposed me to situations that the typical person doesn't experience, and they made a lasting impact on me.

It was sobering to find people dead and to see people dying. I saw life leave people. I watched infants die. I worked accidents where innocent victims were killed because of drunk drivers. You can't witness events like those without them taking a toll on you. When you see an older person die, you can deal with it by telling yourself that's the journey of life. But when you watch an infant or a young child lose his or her life . . . man, it sticks with you. All deaths are tough, but it's really difficult to watch a kid die.

Being a firefighter forced me to stop and consider how fragile life was. I was in my late teens and early twenties at the time. Most people just don't think about dying at that age. You don't really think about the consequences of your actions. At that age, you're kind of sheltered. You see death on television, but it's not nearly the same as seeing it firsthand. And I saw it more times than I would care to count.

My time with the fire department made me question aspects of life. I asked *why* a lot. I wondered about the fairness of life and death. Although those types of questions still come to mind occasionally, I no longer dwell on them; I have learned to trust God and no longer second-guess His motives. But at the time, I struggled with the things I saw.

An Honorable Profession

I have tremendous respect for the firefighters—the men *and* the women—who make sacrifices every day in order to help keep others safe. The twenty-four hours on, forty-eight off schedule sounds great, but twenty-four hours is a long time. That is twenty-four solid hours away from home, away from family. If you think about it, that's four entire months out of the year that firefighters are away from their homes. That's four months a year of not sleeping in their beds. And then they are constantly being awakened during the middle of the night to answer calls. One thing I learned as a firefighter is that there is always something going on out there.

When I graduated from Tennessee Tech through the student-firefighter program in December 2009, I was offered a graduate assistant position at Tech working with the intramural sports program. I took the job and left the fire department in order to begin working on a master's degree, but at the time, I intended to return to firefighting after finishing my graduate degree. As it turned out, God had other plans for me.

I'm still good friends with firefighters in Cookeville. When I had an endorsement contract with Reebok, I was allowed to help design a special workout shoe for the 2012 Games that paid tribute to the 343 firefighters who lost their lives on 9/11. The shoes were red, white, and blue, and they had a big *343* on the sides and *Never Forget 9-11-2001* back toward the heels. Proceeds from sales were designated for the Cookeville Fire Department, and I believe we were able to provide about $30,000 worth of CrossFit equipment for them to have so that they could do CrossFit workouts without having to leave their stations.

I miss working at the fire department, particularly being around the firefighters and the rush that comes with the job. There might even be a day after CrossFit when I go back to working as a firefighter. Who knows? We'll just have to see what God has in store.

CHAPTER 5

INTRODUCTION TO CROSSFIT

WHEN I ENROLLED at Tennessee Tech after quitting baseball and the TRW assembly line, I decided to pursue a degree in exercise science with a concentration in fitness and wellness. I hadn't chosen a career yet, but because I enjoyed working out, I could see myself with some kind of career in sports. I thought I could become a strength and conditioning coach or maybe a personal trainer. One day, I imagined, I might even own a gym.

One of my exercise classes, Training for Performance, was taught by a guy named Chip Pugh. Chip was Tennessee Tech's head strength and conditioning coach, and he was responsible for overseeing the physical development of all the school's athletes. As a part of each class, Chip showed us videos from CrossFit.com, CrossFit's official website. I was working out at the fire department but not following any particular program—just lifting weights and doing exercises I knew from high school. The CrossFit exercises piqued my curiosity, so I started trying some of them.

I liked them.

After I tried a new workout, I'd go back to class and ask Chip questions based on my experiences.

One day after class, Chip said, "You know, you seem pretty interested in this stuff. You need to check into getting a CrossFit Level 1 certification."

I had no idea what that meant. When I asked, Chip told me that a Level 1 certification is the first level of qualifications for working as a CrossFit trainer. I asked Chip what I would need to do to get certified, and he gave me an overview of the process. Then he added a comment that really grabbed my attention: after I received my certification, he might be interested in hiring me to work at his CrossFit Cookeville affiliate or as an assistant in the Tennessee Tech weight room.

The Level 1 trainer course is an introduction to the methods, concepts, and movements of CrossFit. In fourteen hours spread over two days, CrossFit trainers took me and the other members of my certification group through numerous CrossFit workouts to learn the proper techniques and how to coach others on doing CrossFit. Next, I had to accumulate a certain number of hours of experience, so I worked unpaid at a CrossFit facility, training people in workouts.

Two weeks after I received my Level 1 certification, I went to Michigan for a visit. My cousin Darren Hunsucker had just graduated high school, and because of some difficult events in his life, I thought he would benefit from moving to Cookeville.

"I just started doing this thing called CrossFit," I told Darren, "and if you move down, we can open up a gym and teach CrossFit together." I was talking off the top of my head more than anything else. I had no concrete plans for opening a gym and didn't even know what it might involve, but Darren did decide to move and rode back to Tennessee with me.

We made it home to Cookeville around eight or nine at night, and even though we had just spent ten hours in a car, one of us said, "Let's do a workout."

I had bought some bumper plates and had installed a pull-up bar inside Dad's equipment barn, and when we got to Dad's place, Darren and I decided to do 10 rounds of 10 pull-ups and 10 push-ups. Our pull-ups were like half range of motion—just getting our chins close to the bar and not over it. Our attempts at kipping on the pull-ups more closely resembled flailing around. It wasn't the prettiest of workouts, and now it doesn't even seem to me like much of a workout at all, but that was our start.

As the weeks went by, Darren and I gradually increased both the skill and intensity of our workouts. Initially we followed CrossFit's three days on, one day off philosophy, which I had learned during my Level 1 certification. One day we were watching a video of a workout that we wanted to try. But we had already turned in a full workout that day.

"Well, we could try it," I told Darren.

He was game, so we started the second workout. And we finished it.

"We're not dead," I told Darren, and he laughed.

So we decided to add a second workout to our days. Then a third. At that time, the conventional wisdom was that working out multiple times in a day was a big no-no. But we weren't concerned about conventional wisdom; we just wanted to keep improving.

That crazy idea of opening a gym with Darren had never gone away, but it hadn't yet materialized either. We kicked it around occasionally, but that was it. Then, over a span of two or three months, we began to discuss it in a more serious manner. Meanwhile, Darren decided to get his own Level 1 certification, and in the 400-square-foot "gym" we had put together in Dad's barn, we began working as personal trainers with a short list of clients.

Friends of our family owned a gymnastics and cheer-leading studio, and after Darren and I had started working as trainers, they allowed us to use part of their facility for free. We took out a loan to purchase additional equipment and converted the donated space into our new gym. But we didn't have enough money to become an official CrossFit-affiliate gym.

In August 2009 Darren and I opened Power Fitness Gym with our friend David Oaks, who became the co-owner.

Immediately we set out to add more clients. Our advertising campaign started as me texting friends and telling them that my cousin and I were working as personal trainers.

Slowly but surely, our client list grew. Former teammates and friends from the fire department came and worked out with us. Dr. Michael Phillips, a former exercise science professor of mine, and his wife, Amanda, hired us as their personal trainers. As Amanda dropped from a size 10 to a size 4 in seven or eight months, she helped further spread word of what we were doing.

Because we weren't a CrossFit affiliate, we could not teach CrossFit classes, but we did make it known that we were following CrossFit methods. Some days we followed the Workout of the Day (WOD) from CrossFit.com. Other days we made up our own workouts based on the CrossFit programming from our Level 1 training combined with basic exercise physiology I was learning in school. Sometimes Darren and I would watch a video of a CrossFit athlete like Jason Khalipa doing a workout and we'd say, "We should try that."

One of the beauties of CrossFit—and one of the big reasons for its incredible surge in popularity—is that anyone can watch a video of CrossFit athletes doing a workout and then go do the same thing. Beginners most likely won't be able to lift the same amount of weight or complete the workout in the same amount of time, but they can do the same movements and go through the same workout. By comparison, there are very few people who can watch an NFL game on television and then go put on a full set of pads and play. Even for those who can, you'll never be able to fully understand the game the way it's played in the NFL. You just can't replicate the size and speed of NFL players, so you won't truly appreciate the players' abilities.

With CrossFit, the average Joe or Jane—with good coaching on the proper and safe techniques—can do the exact same movements the top athletes do. And because all the CrossFit workouts are scored based on times, reps, or weights, they can compare their results to the elite scores. Even though they might finish in a time five or six minutes slower than the athlete on the video, they still can gain a complete understanding of what the workout involves and what the pros are going through while performing it.

I speak from experience because Darren and I worked out in my dad's barn and compared our numbers to the CrossFit athletes. We also had local competitions with the guys we worked out with and hung out with on weekends. When the video for the 2009 CrossFit Games came out, we immediately watched the entire thing. Then we watched it another three or four times. We thought actually competing on an organized level would be cool and talked about giving it a shot.

In January 2010 we got our chance. When registration for the CrossFit Sectionals qualifying round was announced, Darren and I noted that the Alabama/Tennessee/Mississippi Sectional would be in Huntsville, Alabama, on the weekend before we had planned on taking a spring break trip to

Florida with Jacob Johnson, one of our workout friends. We considered that we could head south a little early and stop in Huntsville so Darren and I could experience what it would be like to compete in an official CrossFit event.

Darren and I decided we would register. I signed up without hesitation. Darren was visiting family in Michigan and told me he would register when he came back to Cookeville.

But Darren didn't sign up.

I couldn't believe it when Darren told me he hadn't registered. He had been the main reason I had signed up, and I wouldn't have if I had known I would have to go compete by myself.

While I was deciding whether to move forward without Darren, there was another even more important agenda item to attend to—proposing!

/// CROSSFIT DEFINED //

BUMPER PLATE
Special weight-lifting plate designed to handle being dropped from overhead. Bumper plates allow athletes to safely handle heavier weights while minimizing damage to the plates, the barbell, the floor, and the athlete.

KIPPING
A full-body movement where an athlete uses feet, hips, and core to allow for a faster and more efficient achievement of a standard movement (like a pull-up). Kipping allows the same amount of work to be done faster, which equals more power.

WORKOUT OF THE DAY

Most CrossFit affiliates post a Workout of the Day (or WOD) for their members to perform. When the members of an affiliate all perform the same workout, athletes can compare performances against each other as well as track their individual improvement since the last time they performed that workout. CrossFit.com posts a WOD, called the "main-site WOD," daily, with every fourth day being a rest day.

///

CHAPTER 6

MY GREATEST GIFT

IN HIGH SCHOOL, I vaguely knew a girl named Hillary Masters. She was two grades behind me, and we didn't really talk much. I could never have guessed this was the woman who would one day become my wife!

Our when-we-met moment occurred on a Saturday morning. I had just gotten off my shift at the fire department and headed over to June Madewell's salon for a haircut. When I arrived, June wasn't there yet. I stayed in my car and noticed that someone else was parked in a car and waiting too. June pulled up a few minutes later, and I got out of the car, greeted June, and held the door open for her. My mom had ingrained in me that I should always hold the door open for women, so I kept the door open and looked toward the other lady sitting in her car. She put on a pair of big sunglasses, got out of the car, and walked toward the door. I recognized her as Hillary Masters.

"Thank you," Hillary said as she entered the salon.

I smiled in return.

I didn't pay attention to this at the time, but Hillary had no makeup on, she was dressed in a T-shirt and shorts, and she hadn't done anything with her hair. After all, it was early on a Saturday morning! When Hillary tells the story, she makes a major deal out of the fact that her hair was a mess. Maybe it's because I'm a guy, but I don't see what's so embarrassing about going to a hair place with your hair messed up. Isn't that why you are going there in the first place—to have your hair done up for you?

We were both there to see June.

Hillary's hair was not quite shoulder length, and June spiked it all over her head to color while I was waiting and watching. We didn't know it then, but June had double-booked us on purpose, hoping to play matchmaker. Hillary later told me that she was becoming wise to June's plot and whispered to her, "This is the last time you will ever do my hair."

It didn't matter to me. I thought Hillary would be attractive no matter how she was dressed or what her hair looked like. And the way she was talking with June, I could tell she had an even more attractive personality.

I had seen Hillary on Facebook through mutual friends,

so I knew how to get ahold of her. I asked if I could call her sometime, and she sent me her phone number. I called and we started talking quite a bit. We didn't date but just spent time having these great conversations. We both had recently ended long relationships, and we talked about those relationships and how neither of us was ready to start dating again.

We continued being "just friends" for four or five months before we decided we both were ready to date again, this time with each other. That was in May 2009.

Hillary's beauty had caught my eye in the beginning— she's gorgeous—but what I liked about her most was how open and honest she was. She had no problem expressing her feelings to me, whether she was happy or upset. I always knew exactly where I stood with Hillary, and she had enough confidence to put me in my place when I needed it. The more time we spent together, the more convinced I became that she was the one for me.

In April 2010, when we had been dating seriously for nearly a year, I was ready to pop the question. I'm not a big planner, but when I was ready to propose, I put a lot of thought into it. I wanted to make it a special moment for a very special person.

Near the end of Hillary's workday on April 27, 2010, I put lilies—her favorite flowers—on her car. I had occasionally left flowers on her car, but this time I included a note that read, *Meet me where I asked you to be my girlfriend.*

There—on the couch in my mother's apartment—I had another bunch of lilies along with another note waiting for her: *Meet me where we met.* June's salon was closed, but I had still more lilies waiting for Hillary outside the door with this note: *The last two places are the past. The next is the future. Meet me where you want to get married.*

Hillary had long ago decided what her ideal wedding would be, and soon after we had become friends, she had told me—not in a hinting way (I'm pretty sure), just as friends—that she wanted to get married at her uncle's home out in the country. Her parents and three of her cousins had held their weddings at the family farm, where the family gathered to celebrate holidays, so it was a special place for her. Hillary had told me how each of her cousins' weddings had been held at different places on the property, but Hillary wanted to get married right at the place where her parents had exchanged vows. I knew the exact spot—under two large chestnut trees—because she had shown it to me.

When Hillary drove up and got out of her car, I stepped out from behind the trees, dropped to a knee, and asked her to marry me. She said yes and started crying. I slipped the ring onto her finger, and she gave me as tight a hug as she could. Then I told Hillary to turn around, and that's when her mother, my mother, my sister, Hillary's best friend, one of her aunts, and one of her cousins came out of hiding. I had alerted them to my plans so they could be there to share in our special moment.

Our moms and Kayla had followed Hillary throughout the scavenger-hunt proposal to take pictures of each stop along the way. Hillary had no idea they were trailing her.

After finding the note and lilies at the salon, Hillary had realized something big was in motion and had called her mom, her sister (who was out of town), and her best friend. "Something is going on!" she told them. "Keep your phone close—I'm freaking out!" When Hillary called her mother, Patty acted like the call had awakened her from a nap. Hillary told Patty that she needed to get up and get to the farm right away, but Patty was already en route with my mom and sister, trying to get there ahead of Hillary!

While Hillary and I were walking over to our families, I revealed the significance of her ring, which her sister, Ali, had helped me with. Ali also had kept the ring for me because I was afraid I would lose it.

Hillary's dad had passed away when she was thirteen, and her mom gave me a diamond she had received from Hillary's dad. That diamond was the middle stone on Hillary's ring. When she looked down at the ring, Hillary "lost it"—her description—and started crying again.

The next day, we sent flowers to June to thank her for double-booking us.

CHAPTER 7

FROM BARN TO GAMES

THE PROPOSAL HAD GONE OFF without a hitch, but the question of the CrossFit Sectional still loomed.

As I thought more about competing at Sectionals without Darren, I almost backed out. But when I told him and our friend Jacob Johnson that I was considering skipping Sectionals, they convinced me to go. Huntsville was a three-hour drive from Cookeville, and from there we would have about six hours to go before reaching our spring break destination of Panama City, Florida. I told Darren and Jacob that I'd go and compete only because it was on the way to Florida, but in my mind I decided that if the first day didn't go well, I'd withdraw and we'd have a head start on spring break.

We pulled into Huntsville on Friday night and drove straight to the site of the competition so we could get the lay of the land. We also wanted to make sure we would know how to get there on time the next morning. It was late when we picked out a motel that met our two criteria: close proximity to the site and cheap. I think our room cost thirty bucks a night, and when we checked in and paid for two nights, the desk clerk took our money from behind bullet-proof glass.

We drove around to our room and noticed bars on the windows. When we unlocked the door and flipped the switch for the main light, the bulb was burned out. With the door still open so we could have outside light shining in, I walked over to the lamp to turn it on. It wasn't plugged in, and I had to move a chair to plug in the lamp. As I moved the chair, a tuna can rolled in the opposite direction. The short leg must have broken off for some other unfortunate guests, and a tuna can had been substituted in the leg's place to keep the chair balanced. When I turned the lamp on, I looked at the back of the chair and noticed what appeared to be a slash made by a knife.

Then Darren shut the door and told us, "Come look at this." A note on the back of the door read, *For your safety, please dead-bolt and lock the door.* We required no further convincing.

We had to have been exceptionally tired to want to close both eyes in that room so we could sleep. Darren and I yanked all the sheets off the bed and slept on the bare mattress in all our clothes, including sweatshirts, so as little skin as possible was exposed to whatever might be on the bed. Jacob wrapped himself in a sleeping bag like a burrito and slept in the chair with the tuna-can leg.

The next morning, with minimal discussion necessary, we voted unanimously to check out of the motel. The motel had a no-refunds policy, but when we said we wanted out, the clerk handed us our second night's money without hassle. Having spent more time there than us, he must not have blamed us for wanting to leave.

I left the motel thinking that the experience there would be the worst part of our weekend in Huntsville, but when we arrived at the qualifier, I wasn't so sure. There were more than eighty athletes signed up for the men's division, and the top fifteen would qualify for Regionals. Based on the comparisons I had made between my own results in my workouts with Darren and the scores put up by some of the top CrossFit athletes, I had set the goal of earning a Regionals berth, but when I saw the other competitors for the first time, I didn't feel like I belonged among them. Some of the other guys looked ridiculous—they were incredible physical specimens.

What have I gotten myself into?

Nowadays, people tell me I look every bit as physically intimidating as the other top CrossFitters, and the funny thing as I think back is that I really didn't look much different then. I was only about five or six pounds lighter, so nothing major. It was a classic example of not seeing yourself from the same perspective with which you view others.

Added into my thought process was the fact that I was still fairly new at CrossFit, that I had never been to any type of CrossFit competition, and that all I knew about how the events worked came from watching the video of the 2009 Games. Finishing in the top fifteen no longer seemed like a realistic goal. I told Darren and Jacob that if I wasn't in the top twenty after the first day, the next motel room we'd be looking for would be somewhere on the road to Florida.

You can imagine my surprise when I won the first workout—3 rounds for time of twenty-five-meter down-and-back sprints (fifty meters total), 10 burpees, and 7 ground-to-shoulders of 155 pounds. I finished in 2:49, which was four seconds ahead of the second-place finisher, Mike McGoldrick.

All right, I thought. *That's a good start.*

The competitor in me doesn't like to admit this, but even if I had finished near the top in the first workout instead of winning, that would have qualified as a moral victory for me.

The second workout consisted of deadlifts and wall-balls—sets of 12, 9, 6, and 3 deadlifts at 275 pounds interspersed with 40, 30, 20, and 10 wall-ball shots at 20 pounds, all for time. I finished second in that event behind McGoldrick. That left us tied for first through two workouts, which took me back to believing a top-fifteen finish was achievable.

Saturday's third and final workout, inspired by and in honor of the Marines, was called The Corps. Marines were on hand to watch the workout, which consisted of 5 rounds for time of a 400-meter run and 25 pull-ups. I finished fourth in The Corps, and McGoldrick came in tenth, leaving me alone in first place at the end of the first day. Drew Shamblin won The Corps to move into second place.

I told Darren and Jacob, "I guess we'll stay and come back for the second day." We picked out a better motel that night.

The first day's workouts had been good ones for me, and I allowed myself to begin considering the possibility that not only could I finish in the top fifteen—I might actually win the Sectional. When I called home to report how I was doing, my mom, Hillary, my sister, and Hillary's sister said they would drive down the next morning for what they hoped would be a victory celebration.

CrossFit has made various changes to its scoring system since I started competing, but at that Sectional, we received one point for each place of our finish in each event. For first place, one point was awarded; for second place, two points; etc. The person with the lowest overall point total at the end of the day Sunday would be the winner. After finishing first, second, and fourth in the first three workouts, I had seven points. Drew Shamblin was in second place with ten points, so I needed to finish within two places of him in the final workout to remain ahead of him. McGoldrick had thirteen points in third place, and there was a good gap between his total and the rest of the field. There are no guarantees in CrossFit, but it looked like it was going to be a three-man competition for first place, and it would have taken almost a complete meltdown for me to not finish in the top fifteen and advance to Regionals.

Sunday's workout, which had been announced Saturday night, was an AMRAP (as many rounds as possible) in fifteen minutes of 5 handstand push-ups (HSPUs), 7 squat snatches at 95 pounds, and 10 reps of twenty-inch box-jumps.

For that final event, we wanted to complete as many reps as we could in the time allowed in order to win. I finished with 247 reps and won the workout by a comfortable margin of 43 reps. Less than twenty-four hours after having wondered why I had bothered to show up, I had earned a spot in Regionals and then some—I had won the Sectional qualifier, edging Shamblin by five points and beating McGoldrick by thirteen.

/// CROSSFIT DEFINED //

BOX-JUMP
Just like it sounds, a box-jump means jumping up onto a box. Standard heights are 24 inches for men and 20 inches for women. Typically both feet have to leave the ground at the same time, and you must reach a fully extended standing position on top of the box.

BURPEE
Simultaneously one of the most hated and revered movements in CrossFit, a burpee consists of dropping down with your chest and thighs resting on the ground, then performing an explosive push-up, landing on your feet, and jumping, achieving full-body extension in the air with arms overhead. Clapping your hands overhead while your feet are off the ground is sometimes included.

DEADLIFT
Lifting a barbell from the ground to waist height.

FOR TIME

Many CrossFit exercises are performed for time, which means a clock is started at the beginning of the workout. At the count of "Three, two, one, go!" the workout begins. The amount of time that has elapsed when you finish the workout is your time. Most CrossFit workouts are either for time or AMRAPs.

HANDSTAND PUSH-UP (HSPU)

Starting in a handstand position (usually up against a wall), lower yourself till the top of your head touches the ground, then push back up into the handstand. Many athletes kip by bending their legs in the down position and then thrusting them upward while pushing back up.

SNATCH

In one fluid movement, lift a barbell from the ground to overhead without pausing at the shoulders. For a squat snatch, simultaneously lower your body into a squat so that you catch the barbell while in the squat position.

WALL-BALL SHOT

A wall-ball is a large medicine ball that you throw against a wall to a target. Standard weights are 20 pounds for men with a target 10 feet off the ground and 14 pounds for women with a 9-foot target. A full squat is required between each throw.

//

A Games Berth—and More

The Southeast Region consisted of seven states: the three from our Sectional (Alabama, Mississippi, and Tennessee) plus Florida, Georgia, North Carolina, and South Carolina. The competition wasn't scheduled until the end of May, on

Memorial Day weekend, which was the last weekend for the Regional competitions. Whereas fifteen had qualified from our Sectional to the next round, only the top four at Regionals would advance to the CrossFit Games.

I didn't know what to expect as I left for Regionals in Jacksonville, Florida. I was one of four Sectionals winners competing, but when I arrived and saw the other athletes, I again suffered that I-don't-belong-here feeling. What helped me most, though, was knowing that by being at Regionals, I had already accomplished my goal for my first year of CrossFit competition. My second-year goal was to qualify for the Games, but that was still an entire year and a couple of months away.

Although fully wanting to win the competition, my mind-set was more *Let's see what we can do here.* Realistically, I wanted to finish in the top half of the nearly seventy who had qualified.

It didn't take me long to discover that I did belong. I tied for fifth in the first event, The Gauntlet—one squat clean every fifty seconds, beginning at 215 pounds and increasing by 10 pounds each lift up to 335 pounds. I maxed out at 325 pounds.

I placed second in the next event, a twelve-minute AMRAP that began with a "buy-in" of 20 handstand push-ups. That meant that once the clock started, we had to complete 20 handstand push-ups before we started counting reps. Once the HSPUs were done, the actual workout consisted of rounds of 20 double-unders, 10 box-jumps (twenty-four inches), and 10 sandbag lunges (ten steps, with a 60-pound sandbag over the back of the shoulders). I completed 461 reps.

The third and final event of the day was a timed workout of 4 rounds consisting of 4 muscle-ups and 16 snatches of a 53-pound kettlebell (with 8 snatches for each arm). I won that event with a time of 3:43 and ended the first day in first place. The point system at Regionals was different from Sectionals; points were still awarded based on how we placed in each event, but unlike at Sectionals, the first-place finisher received 500 points, while the rest of the point values decreased on a sliding scale.

With two events remaining on Sunday, my lead over second place was eighty-seven points, or roughly the difference between first place and twenty-third in one event.

I've always been nervous during competitions, going all the way back to youth baseball, but leading Regionals after the first day made me a nervous wreck that night. I'm more comfortable when I'm behind than when ahead, because when I'm the one everyone is chasing, I start playing games in my mind about having to protect my lead. There was a lot of thinking going on inside my hotel room that night, and much of it came while I would have preferred to be sleeping.

It was a good thing I had a sizable lead because I struggled in Sunday's first event—2 rounds of a 500-meter row and 25 burpees, for time—and placed fourteenth. My time of 5:58.1 was well behind the winning time of 5:33.2 turned in by Nate Schrader. But still, I lost only thirteen points to my closest competitor, Michael Giardina ("Mike G."), and maintained a good lead going into the final event, called The Qualifier—fitting enough for what was at stake. The workout was 8 rounds, for time, of two 145-pound squat snatches, four 145-pound press- or push-jerks, six chest-to-bar pull-ups, and a 200-meter run.

There was a short recovery time of fifty minutes between Sunday's two events. Either workout would have been tough on its own, but with such a limited recovery mixed into the equation, the thought was that the fittest athletes would perform the best over the events. There was little time to dwell on turning in my lowest finish of the weekend in the row-burpee. Still, I did manage to stew a little bit about my disappointing performance in the next-to-last event.

The top twelve individuals were placed in the final heat of the final event, so I knew I would be able to eyeball the closest competitors. A group of us were sitting around and talking while we rested before the final event, including Mike G. and Russell Berger. Both were in the running for the top four. "As long as you don't die in the middle of the workout," Russell told me, "you've pretty much got it locked up."

With my lead, I knew I would need just a decent showing in my heat to qualify for the Games, but CrossFit isn't about doing only what it takes to get by; it's about doing your best and going all out. I can't imagine competing with a just-good-enough mind-set. If I'm there, I'm there to win.

I thought back to a baseball game during my high school days when we had taken a big lead on a team and then watched, almost stunned, as that team came back to defeat us. We had gotten ahead and relaxed, and that wound up costing us a victory. Coach Chaffin chewed us out something good after that game. "You get 'em down," he barked at us, "you keep 'em down!" I learned a lesson that day that stuck with me, and I went into The Qualifier as though I needed to finish first to advance.

The competitors in our heat began to spread out fairly quickly. By the third round, Spencer Hendel and I had broken out ahead of the rest of the pack. By the fourth round, I had taken over the lead from Spencer. As I began my eighth and final round with the squat snatches and press- or push-jerks, I heard the public-address announcer calling out that the top time from the other heats had been 12:32 and then that I was at the 10:30 mark. I wanted to beat that time to win the final event, and I did so, becoming the only competitor to finish the workout in less than twelve minutes, at 11:56.

After the medal ceremony, I sat down for an interview with the CrossFit media. The interviewer pointed out that because I had not only won at Sectionals and Regionals but also because of the margins by which I had won them, expectations would be steeper for me at the Games. No longer, the interviewer told me, would I be advancing to the next round as a relative unknown. He asked how that would impact me.

I quickly informed him that while it might increase the pressure I would feel running up to the competition, it absolutely would not affect my mind-set going in. I felt fortunate that the workouts at the Southeastern Regional had been, for the most part, good workouts for me and that a different set of workouts could have meant a lower finish. Plus, the row-burpees had revealed a weakness I needed to work to correct. There was nothing about winning Regionals that could give me a big head.

The biggest highlight of the weekend came after the competition, when I met Dave Castro, CrossFit's director of training. Dave asked where I was from, and I told him I was from Tennessee. I added that my cousin and I owned a gym there but that we had yet to be able to afford the CrossFit affiliation fees.

"E-mail me on Monday," Dave said. "We'll waive that first year's fee so you guys can be a CrossFit gym."

I was beside myself, not really knowing how to reply to Dave other than "Thank you." I had wanted more than anything to be able to come up with the money to pay for a CrossFit affiliation. Now, what had started as a goal of merely reaching Regionals had turned into a Regionals championship, a berth in the Games, and a free CrossFit affiliation for one year as a gift from none other than Dave Castro himself.

/// **CROSSFIT DEFINED** //

CHEST-TO-BAR PULL-UP

This is just like it sounds—a pull-up where, instead of just getting your chin above the bar, you have to continue pulling until your chest makes contact with the bar.

DOUBLE-UNDER

Jumping rope where the rope must pass two times beneath your feet on every jump.

KETTLEBELL

A heavy metal ball with a handle, used for one- or two-arm swings, cleans, jerks, throws, and any number of other exercises. Working with kettlebells increases grip strength and works all kinds of muscles in the upper and lower body.

KETTLEBELL SWING

Holding the kettlebell with both hands, swing it down and back, between your legs, and then all the way up over your head till you achieve full extension.

MUSCLE-UP

The muscle-up is one of CrossFit's benchmark movements. You start out hanging from a set of gymnastic rings, then pull yourself up and get your body into a position where you're supporting yourself above the rings with your elbows bent. Then push yourself up until your elbows lock. Muscle-ups are typically very difficult for people to master, but once you do, it's an amazing feeling of accomplishment.

PUSH-JERK

With a bar resting at shoulder level, slightly bend your knees and then drive upward using your legs while simultaneously dropping beneath the bar, catching it overhead in a locked-out position before standing all the way back up.

ROW

Rowing in CrossFit means using a rowing machine that keeps track of virtual distance and calories burned. Some workouts specify a certain length (like 500 meters) to row; in others you measure calories.

SQUAT CLEAN

Lift a barbell from the ground to shoulder height, catching it in a full squat position before standing back up. This typically allows athletes to clean heavier weights, though it can be tough to get the hang of at first.

//

CHAPTER 8

WELCOME TO THE GAMES

THE HOME DEPOT CENTER in Carson, California, was a long trip from the barn gym at my dad's place—and in more ways than one.

Only a year after beginning CrossFit workouts with no one but Darren alongside me, I had made it to the CrossFit Games in the sprawling, first-class-all-the-way facility in Southern California. My journey to the Home Depot Center had been only slightly faster than the Games' own journey.

The CrossFit Games began in 2007 with seventy competitors and 150 fans—and the spectator count included the competitors whose events weren't going on at the time—at a place called The Ranch, farther north in California, in

Aromas, south of San Jose. The site literally was a ranch—it belonged to Dave Castro. The first two years, there had been no qualifying rounds. Interested competitors simply needed to show up at Dave's ranch and register. In 2009 Regional qualifiers were created to determine the Games field. When the number of spectators jumped from about 1,300 in 2008 to 4,500 in 2009, the event had outgrown The Ranch and created zoning problems with the city of Aromas.

Those Games at The Ranch are now thought of affectionately by some of the competitors from those years as "the good old days" of the Games, a "Woodstock of fitness," as they are sometimes called. I wish I could have competed at least once at The Ranch because of its history as the original site of the Games. When Darren and I watched the '09 Games video, I visualized myself competing there one day. But it is cool to say that my first Games was the first one at the Home Depot Center.

The Home Depot Center is a 125-acre multiple-venue complex that includes state-of-the-art stadiums for soccer, tennis, track and field, and cycling. The Los Angeles Galaxy and Chivas USA of Major League Soccer play home games there. The United States Tennis Association has a national training center there. USA Cycling and USA Track and Field have official training sites there.

It's a big-time facility, and the fact that the fourth CrossFit Games was moved there demonstrates just how huge the Games had become in such a short time.

The 2010 CrossFit Games competition was scheduled

for three days, Friday through Sunday, July 16–18. I flew to California with Darren that Wednesday, and we made sure to get a better place to stay than we had at the first competition. At Sectionals, we had gotten a room in a *mo*tel. Now we were staying in a *ho*tel, although, still being cost-conscious, we didn't rent a car. Our hotel was a mile from the Home Depot Center, and we walked there each day.

We went over to the Home Depot Center on Thursday afternoon. Walking into the 8,000-seat tennis stadium—the Games' main arena—and seeing the big CrossFit logo on the floor, then walking past the pull-up rigs that had been constructed, was a welcome-to-the-Games moment for me. I looked up into the rows of empty seats and imagined what it would be like the next day when fans filled those seats, and it was a pretty cool scene in my mind. I'd been inside big stadiums as a fan, but I had never performed in a stadium that came close to comparing to that one.

When the competitors began gathering for the pre-Games meeting, I again got that feeling of not belonging. That's difficult to explain, because after winning Sectionals and placing first in what had turned out to be a tough Regionals, "the kid from Tennessee" had been labeled a contender to watch.

Except I didn't view myself that way. Again, as had been the case at Sectionals, I didn't see myself as others saw me. More specifically, I didn't see myself as I was seeing the other competitors. At the athletes' meeting, I was almost starstruck as I recognized guys I had watched work out on videos, such as Jason Khalipa, the 2008 Games winner; Chris Spealler, who had already become a CrossFit legend and fan favorite; James FitzGerald, who had won the first Games; and Mikko Salo, the 2009 Games champion and reigning Fittest Man on Earth, whom I had watched on video any number of times as he impressively earned that title.

For me, seeing those guys in person was almost like seeing movie stars up close and personal for the first time. Except unlike with movie stars, I was going to be competing alongside them—and *against* them—the next day. And physically they looked like beasts.

I caught myself picking out specific competitors and thinking, *I'm not as fast as he is.* Or *I've seen him move on video, and I don't move like that.* Or *He's better at some of these workouts than I am.*

I didn't feel like I belonged in the same room as the top CrossFitters, and I sure didn't want to be that rookie guy walking up to them and introducing myself by saying, "I've watched you on TV!"

Then, on Friday morning my dad called to inform me that I was on the front page of the Games website. Because of the interviews I had done since winning the Southeast Regional, I knew that no matter how much I wished I could, I was not going to be able to quietly sneak into the Games. I've always much preferred pursuing the target instead of wearing one, and I was nervous because that was not going to be the case in my first Games. And my dad was on the phone reminding me.

"Don't tell me that," I said.

"No pressure," he replied, laughing.

The Games opened on Friday morning with competitions between teams from the top-ranked CrossFit affiliates and events for the Masters (older age group) competitors, so my first event wasn't scheduled until that evening. One of the defining characteristics of the CrossFit Games is the element of the unknown. We weren't told what the first workout would be until we were in the warm-up area moments before being introduced to the crowd and making our way onto the floor for our respective heats: a couplet of muscle-ups and 135-pound squat snatches. The workout was 9 reps of each movement, then 7 reps of each, and then five (9-7-5 in CrossFit-speak). Squat snatches give a lot of people trouble, but they had come relatively easy for me, so I liked having that movement in the first event. I noticed most competitors coolly walking out onto the stadium floor as their names were announced, but I was so pumped to be there that I ran.

Dave Castro introduced each of the athletes, and he introduced me as "Rich *Fraw*-ning Jr." instead of "*Froh*-ning." I've since learned that Dave has a tendency to mispronounce names, and I wonder if it's his way of messing with people a little mentally during competitions. Additionally, I was still getting used to having *Junior* added to my name. I shared my dad's name, but I wasn't called Junior growing up. When I registered for Sectionals, there was a box for *suffix* after the last name on the entry form, and without really thinking about any future ramifications, I added *Jr.* there. I had no idea that would be the beginning of me being referred to as "Rich

Froning Jr." But, hey, "*Fraw*-ning," "Junior"—whatever they wanted to call me, I was just glad to be dashing out onto the Home Depot Center floor as a Games competitor.

That first trip out in front of the fans was a lot like that Friday-night-lights feeling I experienced going onto the field before a game during my brief high school football career. It was an amazing feeling—surreal.

But because we went straight from introductions into the first event, there wasn't much time for feelings. I had to quickly get into workout mode.

Exceeding Expectations

The time to beat from an earlier heat of the muscle-up/squat snatch couplet had been set at 4:01, and the workout went well for me. I could tell that Neal Maddox was having a good workout in my heat too, but because of where we were positioned for the final round of snatches, I couldn't see how I was measuring up to him. I finished the workout in 3:47 to beat the previous best, and I dropped the bar and turned to my right to see that Neal had just finished too. As we made our way toward each other to shake hands, I saw that he had beaten me by one second. Dave Castro announced, "The two fastest times of the night!" and he shook my hand.

James FitzGerald came up to me when we were back in the athletes' area. "You're my dark horse to win this thing," he said.

"Thanks," I said. My thoughts that went unsaid were *What? You can't say that. You've won the CrossFit Games, not me.*

That couplet was the only workout Friday, and I watched in the final heat as Chris Spealler beat both Neal and me with a time of 3:29. At the end of the first day, after one event, I was in third place.

By placing that high, I earned a spot in the final heat for Saturday's first event at the track-and-field stadium—two events in one, scoring-wise. The first was a pyramid double Helen. Usually Helen is 3 rounds of a 400-meter run, 21 kettlebell swings at 55 pounds, and 12 pull-ups. This workout was also 3 rounds, but the first round was a 1,200-meter run, 63 kettlebell swings, and 36 pull-ups. The second round was an 800-meter run, 42 kettlebell swings, and 24 pull-ups. The third round was the standard 400-meter run, 21 kettlebell swings, and 12 pull-ups. That would be followed by a second workout for separate scoring: ninety seconds for maximum weight of a shoulder-to-overhead lift. Any lift was allowed, so long as the weight started on your shoulders and ended up locked out overhead.

I completed the run, swings, and pull-ups in 18:10 (which would be good enough for sixth place in that event) and was exhausted as I walked to where the bars were set up for the shoulder-to-overhead. Just to establish this now, the default description for how I feel after every workout at the Games is "exhausted." Each event is an exhausting workout on its own, so imagine stacking one exhausting workout on top of another on top of another, and that is how it feels to compete in the Games.

Adding to the difficulty of the overhead lift was that it came mere seconds after finishing the pull-ups, which had come on the heels of the kettlebell swings. Both pull-ups and kettlebells just about rip your arms out of their sockets, so lifting for max weight would have been somewhat easier if it had come directly after running instead of the back-to-back movements using the arms. But when Dave sets the Games workouts, the phrase "somewhat easier" is not a consideration.

We were given a minute and a half for our max lift on the overhead, and the weights were set up at 135 pounds to begin. With my arms feeling wobbly as I struggled to keep balance, I jerked the weight and almost missed it, but I did manage to lock it out overhead and then set the bar back on the rack. I bent over to pick up the first plate to add to the bar for a heavier lift, and when I stood up, the venue was spinning. Putting the weight on the bar was like playing one of those video games where you're trying to shoot an enemy airplane down but first you have to get the radar locked in, and the target keeps moving and you can't lock in the radar. That bar looked like it was moving as I tried to lock in my radar so I could add the extra plates.

I managed only a disappointing 245-pound max in the overhead. In my preparations for the Games, I had jerked 315. Even considering the run, swings, and pull-ups, I thought I should have been able to lift 275 or 285. I finished tied for thirteenth in the event.

Fortunately for me, Chris Spealler, who had won Friday night's event and was second in the Helen event, placed only twenty-sixth in the overhead. Neal Maddox, who was in the spot ahead of me after Friday, dropped back on Saturday morning.

Graham Holmberg led after the overhead, with Matt Chan next. I was third, with Chris Spealler behind me in fourth. When I saw my standing, I felt a little bit as though I had gotten away with one because of my struggles in the overhead. But that also served as in-person proof of what I had observed about Games competition: not having a meltdown can be more important than winning an event. The Games rewards across-the-board ability. You don't have to be the absolute best at anything to win as long as you're *among* the best in everything.

We had about a six-hour break until our next event, which gave me an opportunity to go up to the top of the stadium and just kind of hang out and chill in an area where the fans could walk around. The stadium was about half-filled that year; now that the stadium is packed out each year and the athletes have become more recognizable, it's too difficult to go to that area because it's so crowded. These days, the Games officials have set up an area where the athletes can still be accessible for fans, but with barriers erected so they can do their postworkout cooldowns and warm up for the next events.

Event 3, in the late afternoon, was a seven-minute AMRAP workout consisting of seven 351-pound deadlifts, a sprint across the stadium floor, 14 pistols, 21 double-unders, and then a sprint back across the stadium to begin another round.

I didn't have a jump rope and had to borrow one from Mike G. Lesson learned from my first Games: when packing while not knowing what the events will be, take all your equipment with you.

The deadlifts/pistols/double-unders is a tough workout because it combines pure strength (deadlifts), agility and coordination (pistols), and a gymnastics movement (double-unders).

Austin Malleolo had turned in the best performance in the earlier heats, completing 5 full rounds and getting through the 14 pistols in the sixth round before the time cap expired.

Early on in my heat, I could see that Spealler—who was next to me on my left—was fast in the pistols and especially in the double-unders. I was doing well in those, but I wasn't getting through them as quickly as Spealler. However, I was making up good time on him in the deadlifts. With a little more than a minute left, I felt like I was beginning to take a small but sure lead on Chris. By that time, the "sprint" across the stadium floor had been reduced to a jog, and I made it back to the deadlifts to start my sixth round ahead of Spealler. I wasn't able to complete the deadlifts unbroken, but I could see him noticeably slowing on his lifts. When I headed back across to the pistols/double-unders area, I glanced over my left shoulder and saw Chris still at the weights.

I began my pistols, and Spealler never appeared beside me

to begin his. I made it through all 14 pistols and picked up the jump rope, but the seven-minute time limit ended before I could do one rep. I had matched Austin Malleolo's total to tie him for first place in the event. Just one double-under and I would have won the event outright.

We had no idea how many events there would be at those Games. Instead, at the conclusion of each event, we were told where we needed to be next and at what time. When I was leaving the floor after the deadlifts/pistols/double-unders, the public-address announcer informed us and the crowd that there would be another event that night and that the workout would be announced in twenty minutes.

Back in the competitors' area, I learned that Graham Holmberg had tied for third in the deadlifts/pistols/double-unders event to keep his overall lead and that I had moved up to second, one point ahead of Matt Chan and fourteen points ahead of Chris Spealler.

During the short break, the men's field was cut from forty-five to twenty-four—only the top twenty-four athletes would be advancing to the next round. The next event was announced to the crowd, but not to us. All the athletes were kept in an area underneath the stadium where we couldn't understand what was being said over the PA system. When the athletes for the first heat went out to compete, they were informed of the details of the workout, but the rest of us had no way of finding out until it was time for our heats.

The fourth event was the Sandbag Move.

Learning what the Sandbag Move consisted of gave me a shot of confidence because that event was in my wheelhouse. It was just work like I had done growing up on Mom and Dad's land. When I won my heat and finished second for the event behind Tommy Hackenbruck, I overtook Graham (who tied for sixteenth) for the overall lead going into the final day.

Needless to say, I was no longer simply trying not to finish last.

This could happen! I told myself.

Back at the hotel, before falling asleep for a surprisingly solid night of sleep considering what was ahead the next day, I thought back to the Sandbag Move and how it seemed like the event had been selected so that I could do well.

Maybe I'm supposed *to win this!*

/// CROSSFIT DEFINED //

JERK
A weight-lifting movement where you move a barbell from your shoulders to overhead in one sudden movement while dropping below the bar to catch it in a locked-out position before standing back upright.

PISTOL
A one-legged squat. You have to keep your balance while squatting all the way down on one leg, keeping your other leg off the ground the whole time. Usually you alternate legs when doing pistols.

//

On the Verge

Event 5 on Sunday morning was a short workout but a killer nonetheless: three cleans of 205 pounds and four ring handstand push-ups, with 7 rounds for time. Ring handstand push-ups are tricky. Gymnastic rings are set a few inches off the ground, hanging from a bar overhead. You have to put your hands in the rings, then kick yourself up into an inverted position while doing your best to hold your hands steady as the rings are trying to move all over the place. Then you have to lower yourself down till your head touches the ground, then push back up to a locked-out position. The movement requires both strength and balance, and needless to say, it's incredibly difficult. We had to do 28 reps—4 reps times 7 rounds—of ring HSPUs in that workout.

The top eight athletes through the first five events were in the third and final heat; the best time of the first two heats was 4:57 by Ben Smith.

I got off to a good start, with Spealler again next to me, but by about the fifth round, my shoulders were Jell-O. I was handling the cleans well, but my fatigued shoulders were slowing me down on the ring HSPUs. When I grabbed the rings and flipped upside down, I had to partially wrap my feet around the ropes to help keep my body vertical. I lost ground to Chris over the final 3 rounds, and he and Graham—who was competing on the opposite side of the setup, where I couldn't keep track of how he was doing—wound up obliterating the previous best time.

Graham finished in 4:26, one second ahead of Chris. Although they finished almost a minute ahead of me—my time was 5:21—I still managed to place fourth in the event. The fact that I was fourth and so far behind Graham and Spealler tells how dominant they were on the cleans and ring HSPUs.

With each place representing one point in the totals, every spot seemed doubly important on Sunday compared to the previous two days. I had maintained my hold on first place with twenty-nine points, but Graham had closed the gap between us to only six points. Matt Chan was in third place with fifty-four points, so there was a good margin between Graham and me and the rest of the field.

The Masters and Team competitions were wrapping up on Sunday also, and while the final events for those divisions were held, we had about three hours to recover from the cleans and ring HSPUs, eat a little bit, try to relax, and then warm up again.

Another round of cuts reduced the total number of competitors in our locker room to thirty-two—sixteen men and sixteen women.

I looked around the room and again took note of how many of those remaining were athletes I had watched on the videos. I sat off in one corner of the room, partly to stay somewhat isolated in my thoughts and partly because even though everyone had been accepting of me in my first Games, I still felt a sense that I was in *their* competition. I didn't want to do anything that would make me look like an idiot rookie.

I think just about every type of mental preparation was on display in that room. Some were joking around with others; some were making small talk in small groups; some were moving around the room trying to keep their bodies loose; some were off by themselves listening to music through earbuds. Everybody had his or her own way of staying ready.

The secrecy of the workouts was one of the distinguishing characteristics of the 2010 Games, and there was no way of trying to anticipate what the next workout might be. I was hoping for a one-rep max of clean-and-jerk or snatch—or something along those lines—because I knew how my numbers compared to some of the others' numbers in those movements. I knew I could hang with them in that type of event. Plus, a short workout like one of those wouldn't be as painful. A one-rep max doesn't hurt nearly as much as a twelve-minute workout of burpees, climbing a wall, handstands, and overhead squats, or some combination of movements like that. Hoping to be assigned a single-rep, max-weight type of workout was unrealistic, but at least my mind enjoyed considering the possibility that the next workout wouldn't be torture.

The group for the first women's heat left, and when the competitors for the next heat were called, none of the first group returned to our room. But we did hear some of them yelling outside our area. Obviously some were upset with their workouts. I think hearing their reactions got into the heads of some of the people in the room.

Also, the fact that it had been about half an hour since the first group had left made it clear that the final event wouldn't be a short one-max rep as I had hoped. On the contrary, it seemed it would be a monster of a workout.

That's when the *What's going on out there?* thoughts started running laps inside my mind. And of course, because being in the top six places of the men's division positioned me in the final group, I had to entertain those thoughts all the way up until those of us in the final heat were called.

Our group of six was in the room for about three hours before being called to our heat. We were allowed no contact with the outside world—no TVs, no phone calls, no text messages—and that isolation made things more difficult mentally. We had no clue what was taking place on the stadium floor and no idea what was coming.

When the call finally did come and we were making our way through the tunnel from the locker room to the floor, those of us who had been competing shirtless because of the warm weather started removing our shirts. Dave Castro stopped us. "Leave your shirts on," he said. "It's pretty dang hot out there."

I slipped back into my shirt. *Why do we need our shirts? If it's hot, we won't want to be wearing shirts.*

When we walked through the curtain that had shielded us from the floor, I could see enough equipment had been set up for multiple workouts. The final event would be a triplet—three workouts back-to-back-to-back. That's why there had been so much time between when one group of competitors left the locker room and the next group was called out for its heat.

Most important, all three workouts would be scored separately. That meant there would be three separate point totals from the final event added to our overall scores. A full one-third of our overall point totals would be handed out in the next thirty minutes or so. That made my six-point lead feel even smaller.

Making things more "fun" for us was that each workout within the triplet would be revealed in stages. After we finished the first workout, we would be given a short break while Dave explained the next one to us.

The first workout was 3 rounds of 30 release push-ups and 21 overhead squats of 95 pounds with a wall rope climb between each element. There was a seven-minute cap. As soon as Dave finished the description, he said, without any fanfare or warning, "Three, two, one, go!" He caught us by surprise with that, and we all just kind of stood there for a split second before realizing it was time to begin.

I was glad we were doing release push-ups instead of handstand push-ups, and I liked hearing about the overhead squats because those are good for me.

It didn't take long to realize why Dave had recommended we wear T-shirts. When I dropped to begin my push-ups, I felt the heat coming off the stadium floor. It was midafternoon with a temperature of probably eighty degrees, but because of the bright sunlight, it was well over a hundred degrees on the black rubber mats on the floor. I didn't see this until watching the Games later, but Matt Chan had a great idea that I made note of to steal down the road: while the rest of us were doing our push-ups in front of our wall, Matt did his to the side in the shade cast by the wall.

I was the first back to the wall after the squats—but barely, and I was going all out. I wasn't concerned about keeping anything in reserve for the rest of the triplet. To save a second or two, when I reached the top of the twelve-foot wall, I decided not to use the rope to descend the other side. Instead, I jumped off the top and did a free fall to the floor. That turned out to be not such a good idea, because I landed hard. If I had been in an Olympic gymnastics competition, the announcers sure wouldn't have said that I stuck my dismount.

Again, I was the first to the wall after the second round of push-ups, but that time I took the slower and less jarring trip to the ground with the assistance of the rope. The rubbery feeling in my arms appeared in my third round of push-ups. Halfway through that round, I had to start lying flat on the hot mat after each push-up and sliding my arms forward to give them a break.

Right after I started my final round of squats, Dave announced that I could become the first athlete to complete the entire workout. That was the first indication that no one in the first two heats had finished the push-ups/wall climbs/overhead squats. There was my motivation to finish, because that would mean that I had won the event and picked up the one first-place point. I completed my last rep of the squats with about twenty seconds remaining. I knew I still was leading everyone in my heat, and all I had to do was climb the wall one more time. I made it to the top okay, but I briefly lost my footing against the wall and had to catch myself so I wouldn't slide back down. I made it over the top and touched down on the other side with five seconds to spare. As I did, Graham Holmberg, positioned next to me, was making his way up on the push-ups side of the wall.

I couldn't tell then what place Graham finished in (it was sixth overall), but I knew that I had won the event and had added at least a few points to my lead over him.

That's all I knew as Dave began to describe the second segment: 3 rounds of 30 toes-to-bar and 21 ground-to-overheads with 95 pounds, with another seven-minute cap.

That break we would have between segments? It turned out to be about only twenty seconds before Dave again said, "Three, two, one, go!"

Perhaps I had expended too much energy on the push-ups and overhead squats. The problem is, when you don't know what workout is coming next, it's difficult to "save yourself" for the ensuing segments. You just have to compete the best you can and hope that somewhere deep inside, you'll be able to find something, some spark kindled from all those hours in the gym preparing for the Games.

I was the last of the six in my heat to finish the first round of toes-to-bar. I felt like I was just flailing, trying to get my toes up to the bar. And then when I made it to the weights, my forearms were taxed. Attempting to do the reps unbroken wasn't a consideration. It was simply pick the bar up, do a rep, and drop it—whatever I had to do to get through them.

When time was called on the seven-minute cap, I was lifting my fifth rep on the second round of ground-to-overheads. I knew I hadn't done well, but without the results being announced, I had no idea where I stood. I thought I might have been last in my heat, and Graham, next to me, might have finished first. But I couldn't know how many points he had picked up on me going into the final segment. Even if I had known, I'm not sure how well I would have been able to process the information. My brain was fried.

Dave started right in revealing the final segment: 5 over-the-wall burpees (with a burpee and climbing a six-foot wall counting as one) and then 3 rope climbs of twenty feet. The workout was 3 rounds with a twelve-minute time limit, whichever came first.

Then Dave said for the final time, "Three, two, one, go!"

They might have been the worst burpees I've ever done. I was slow going over the wall each time too, hooking my arms over the top and then working my chest up so I could pull the rest of my body over to the other side. I felt awful. Just awful. All I was trying to do was hang with Graham to my right. Assuming I had a slight lead over Graham, I wanted to make sure I didn't let him get out ahead of me.

Graham and I finished our first round of burpees and wall climbs at the same time, less than a minute in, and I could look down the row of competitors and see that we were the first two headed to the rope climb. The walk to the rig was about twenty feet.

When I reached my rope, I bent over and put my hands on my knees, trying to catch my breath and give my body a few seconds off for needed recovery. Graham also was taking a quick break next to me.

I don't really remember what I was thinking. For all I know, in the physical and mental state I was in as I stood upright to grab the rope, I might not have even been thinking at all. But I do know what I should have been thinking.

Uh-oh.

/// CROSSFIT DEFINED //

CLEAN
Lifting a barbell from the ground to a rack position at shoulder height in one fluid movement.

CLEAN-AND-JERK
A clean followed immediately by using your legs to thrust the bar to a locked-out position overhead.

GROUND-TO-OVERHEAD
Lift a barbell from the ground to a locked-out position overhead by whatever means necessary. You can snatch it or clean-and-jerk it; just get it up there.

HAND-RELEASE PUSH-UP
A push-up where you pause at the bottom with your chest on the ground and lift both hands off the ground.

FIRST

OVERHEAD SQUAT
A full squat performed while holding a barbell over your head.

TOES-TO-BAR
Hanging from a pull-up bar, raise your lower body until your toes are
touching the bar.

//

CHAPTER 9

THE ROPE

I REACHED UP and grabbed the rope, pulled myself up, and started to wrap my feet around the rope.

Nothing.

I slid back down to the mat.

Not once while Dave Castro was describing the final workout of the Games had I paused to consider that I did not know how to climb the rope.

When I was growing up, there had been a rope in my dad's barn. "Don't use your feet," my dad would tell me when I climbed it. "That's that sissy way. Use your arms."

As a kid, with much less body weight to raise, I could climb a rope using only my arms fairly easily. But now, at this final stage of the Games, with Jell-O for arms and shoulders trying to lift 190 pounds, Dad's non-sissy method wasn't going to work.

I backed away and removed the gymnastic grips from my hands. Then I stepped back to the rope, grabbed it again, and managed two tugs before dropping down.

I stood there with my right hand on the rope.

How am I going to do this?

I tried again and made it maybe four feet up the rope, legs flailing, before sliding back to the ground. I looked over at the other five competitors. They were clamping their feet onto the rope somehow and using their legs for leverage as they climbed. I gripped the rope and tried to slip a foot into it. I couldn't.

I'm doing something wrong here.

"Use your feet, Rich! Use your feet!"

Normally during competition, fans' voices don't stand out. I'm so zoned into each workout that all I hear is a muffled crowd noise. I'll hear the music, but afterward I usually can't remember what songs were playing. But now, standing almost helplessly beside the rope and seeing everyone else in my heat—especially Graham Holmberg, next to me—making their rope climbs as they neared completion of their first rounds, I could hear fans shouting instructions to use my feet. Some sounded almost as frustrated as I was.

I looked into the front rows of the stadium. One fan had actually removed a shoelace from his shoe and was holding it with one hand and using the fingers on his other hand to demonstrate how I should use my feet.

I knew I needed to use my feet, but my mind was so fatigued and frustrated that I couldn't process how to do it—not even by watching the others or the fan climbing his shoelace with his fingers.

After a couple of minutes, Graham completed his third rope climb and walked back to the wall to begin his second round. Chris Spealler was ahead of him, starting his rope climbs for the second time. I still hadn't made it to the top once.

Yet again I grabbed the rope and tried to work one of my legs around it somehow, but I couldn't position my foot to where I could try to hoist myself. Again I stepped back and stared at that silly rope.

Why can't I get up there?

Even watching the other guys and trying to pick up on their methods, I still couldn't figure it out. I'd take note of how Graham was climbing his rope, but it just wouldn't click with me.

I was learning the hard way that there is more technique to climbing a rope than meets the eye. The rope climb is a body-weight movement, and my arms and shoulders were basically gone. But even though we were in the final event of the Games, I knew I still possessed the physical capacity to do it. And that's what was so frustrating. I knew I could do it if I knew the proper technique, that if I could use my legs along with my arms, the difference would be night and day. But I didn't know how. The Games had caught me unprepared.

More than half of the twelve-minute cap had ticked off the stadium clock.

I bent over and dipped my hands into an orange bucket of chalk. My hands were burning from the previous attempts on the rope, and I needed something—anything—to help with my grip. I took a few steps back, looked up to the top of the rope—not just at the rope, but to the top of it—stepped forward, waved my arms from side to side a few times to try to loosen my muscles, quickly grabbed the rope, and jumped.

I started climbing, legs kicking wildly. It was all up to my arms and shoulders, and I finally was getting near the top. Another few pulls, and I had made it at last. I reached up, tapped the bar, and then as I tried to place my left hand back on the rope, my arms and shoulders screamed, *No more*. My hands simply could not hold my body weight on the rope.

That's when the twenty-foot fall started, and that's when both hands decided to let go because they didn't want to lose any more skin to the rope than they already had. I couldn't feel the pain at the time because of the adrenaline, I guess, but I hit the ground hard enough that I later had to have my feet x-rayed. I had bruised both heels and my tailbone when I thudded against the mat. I also hurt my neck when I slammed into the chalk bucket, but I didn't even think about that at the time.

The remaining five minutes of the event are a blur. Most of the details I now know come from the television coverage—and yes, I've seen the video of the rope climb too many times.

Chris Spealler touched the ground at the end of his final rope climb at the 8:32 mark, which was two minutes ahead of the fastest time from the previous heats. Graham was back on the burpees and wall climbs. I assumed he was on his final round. And still, I had made it to the top of my rope only once.

Despite my many failures on the rope, I wouldn't quit. There was no giving up. When I was a kid, my parents wouldn't allow quitting. Anytime there didn't seem to be a way to get something done, they made sure I kept going until I did find a way. That work ethic had gotten me to the Games, and it was keeping me going despite my frustration.

Besides, not knowing where I stood in the overall competition and understanding that every rep completed could significantly impact the final standings, I *couldn't* quit. I never entered an I-can't-do-this mode. Instead, my mind-set the entire time was *I'm going to figure this out. I've got twelve minutes to fight with this rope.*

It *was* a fight too.

With less than three minutes remaining and Graham back next to me and climbing the rope in his final round, I gave it yet another go. One of the TV announcers commented that I was "bicycle kicking" my way up toward the top of the rope. The only way he could have more accurately described my technique, if you want to call it that, would have been to add the word *desperately*.

I again made it near to the top, but again my arms and shoulders ran out of steam. I stopped climbing and wrapped my thighs around the rope, not to climb but to hold my position. That momentary break for my arms and shoulders gave me a chance to pause before making the one big push that allowed me to tap the top of the climb for the second time.

I slid down the rope to a few feet from the floor, then fell the rest of the way and rolled over onto my back on the mat. I guess the mat had to be hot on that end of the stadium too, but I don't remember feeling it. I formed an imaginary pistol with my right hand and put it up to my forehead to signal that I was done. Mentally and physically, just done.

Two and a half minutes remained in the workout, and I needed every place I could gain in that time. I forced myself to get up and grab the rope again, ignoring the pain in my hands. This time I was finally able to sort of grip the rope between my crossed ankles, giving my exhausted arms just enough help to get me to the top for the third time. It wasn't pretty, but I got it done. I managed to control my descent a little better that time but still ended up dropping to the floor from about ten feet up, collapsing to my hands and knees as I landed. With just fifteen seconds left before the time cap expired, I struggled to my feet, ran to the wall, and managed one burpee and one wall climb before time was called.

I leaned back against the wall, more glad the event was finally over than anything else. I had no idea how I had placed. I knew I hadn't done well compared to the others in my heat, but there was no way to know how I had matched up with those in the first two heats.

I hoped I had somehow managed to keep the lead. But I would have to wait to find out.

And wait.

And wait.

Three Points over Three Days

We were ushered directly from the stadium floor to the locker room for drug tests. Those of us who were the likely top three finishers plus a few others who were randomly selected had to remain there together until we had each given a urine sample. We had expended so much energy and lost so much body fluid through sweating that it was hard for us to pee. We were not allowed to drink anything, either, to avoid diluting our urine. We were back there, trying to pee, for an hour or an hour and a half. And still, none of us knew where we had finished.

Even when the drug tests had been completed, we weren't clued in to who had won. That information was being held for the grand announcement at the awards ceremony. So I stood out on the stadium floor, anxiously waiting to find out if I had won. And then I saw the oversize ceremonial $25,000 check that would be presented to the winner. Our view of the check was supposed to be blocked, but I had just enough of an angle to make out the name on the check: Graham Holmberg.

Instantly, I went from thinking, *I could win this—I'm going to win this*, to feeling like a tire that had had all its air released at once. That was the most deflating moment I've ever experienced.

Graham had beaten me by three points. That's three places over nine events held over three days. In the final event, Graham had placed fifth, and I was twelfth. If I had just been able to complete that final workout before the time cap, if I had just known how to climb that stupid rope, that would have given me more than enough points to win.

In my wife's photo album of the 2010 Games, there is a picture of me bent over as the silver medal was placed around my neck.

I'm smiling.

It's a fake smile.

Less than a year earlier, I had watched the Games on video with my cousin and had thought it would be fun to give competing a shot. When I entered the qualifiers leading up to the Games, I had hoped to do well but had never expected to win. Yet I had won. But in the final competition, I had come up short. And now here I was, standing on the medal platform, to the right of and a little lower than Graham Holmberg, one of the guys I had watched on that video, being announced as the runner-up. The only person who had finished ahead of me, and by only three points at that, was the Fittest Man on Earth. And I had to fake a smile.

During the course of the weekend, my expectations had changed. My perspective had changed.

I had changed.

Sitting in the locker room before the final event, in first

place, I had begun to think, *I can win this thing.* That's when my pride started to kick in. I had gone to my first Games hoping only to make my family and my friends back home proud. But in a matter of only six events, making others proud had yielded to my own pride.

Then, even faster, I had fallen off the rope. That verse from Proverbs about pride going before a fall? I experienced that. I had gone from "the kid from Tennessee" to the top of the Games leaderboard and then to flat on my back on the mat. The end of that roller-coaster ride was difficult to stomach because there was one thing other than the rope that I wasn't prepared for: handling my own pride.

CHAPTER 10

AFTERMATH

"Why do you do what you do?"

I looked at my good friend Chip Pugh without answering immediately. "I don't know," I replied, unable to find a better response.

"Think about it," he said. "Then get back to me."

Six months had passed since the 2010 CrossFit Games, and the positive momentum that would be expected from finishing second in my debut Games was not around. In fact, it had never shown up.

I feared my competitive CrossFit aspirations had vanished almost as soon as they had appeared out of nowhere. What had started as little more than a whim had quickly become my everything, an all-consuming drive to prove myself in CrossFit competitions.

Chip's question wouldn't go away. It still was echoing in my mind a few days later when another close friend and mentor, Donovan Degrie, asked me a series of pointed questions in a car ride home from a CrossFit seminar.

"If you were to die today," he asked, "would you go to heaven?"

"Of course," I answered.

"Why do you think that?" he asked.

"Because I believe in Jesus, and I believe that He died for our sins."

From there, our conversation launched into the various ways people tend to view God. Some view God as a fatherly type, Donovan explained. Some see Him as a great punisher. Some look at Him as a Santa Claus of sorts. I had never really thought about how I viewed God, and as Donovan talked, I recognized that I probably fell into the God-as-Santa-Claus column. My prayers, I realized, all seemed to revolve around what I wanted God to give me.

When we arrived home from the three-and-a-half-hour trip, I said good-bye to Donovan until our next workout together. But Donovan's questions stayed with me. As with what Chip had asked, the questions that Donovan posed kept elbowing their way to the front of the line in my mind, insisting, demanding that they be answered.

I began asking myself questions.

What is my purpose?

Why am I here?

Why do I do CrossFit?

Who am I?

What *am I?*

Gradually the answers began revealing themselves to me, and I didn't like them. I had become in my own mind what people had come to know me as since my big splash in my first Games—Rich Froning the CrossFitter.

What kind of legacy am I going to leave if I die? Is it just CrossFit? Is that what people are going to remember me for?

And then there was the one question that really shook me.

Is CrossFit what my family will remember me for?

Weakness into Strength

I attack weaknesses. A good CrossFit athlete must, because CrossFit has a way of locating and exposing weaknesses. Sometimes it does so brutally. It just so happened that by virtue of the manner in which I had left the 2010 Games as the runner-up, I had a weakness obvious to anyone who watched or read about the Games.

Immediately after returning home from the Games, I had taken out my laptop, pulled up Google, and typed in *CrossFit rope climb* in the search box. All it took was a couple of minutes of watching one video to see an experienced climber properly use his feet, and I knew what I needed to do to climb a rope. I tend to be good at quickly picking up on techniques and concepts. In fact, that's one of the more unknown keys to doing well at the Games. During competition, the best athletes look to the other top competitors to see how they are doing a workout and then adopt their technique. Even if you're already good at a particular workout, you can still look at the others to see if there is a better, more efficient way than your good way. Every place matters at the Games, and that makes every rep, every second, and every pound important.

It certainly was much easier to figure out the rope climb in the comfort of my home than it had been in the middle of competition, in a daze from being physically and mentally worn out and with a couple hundred fans yelling at me. Not to mention that guy holding the shoestring.

We were home only a couple of days before we drove up to Michigan to visit family. At Darren's family's home, there is a big, sprawling shade tree. From one of its thick lower branches hangs a tire swing. From another, a rope. I studied the rope from a distance for a few seconds. The top of the rope looked like it stood fifteen to eighteen feet above the ground. Not quite twenty feet, but close enough for what I needed to do.

Hey, if you're going to attack your weaknesses, there's no better time to get right back on the rope than the first opportunity presented.

There was no *Let's give this a try*. Or *Let's see if I can do this*.

What I told myself instead was a determined *I'm gonna go do this*.

I grabbed the rope, and with my feet helping my arms and shoulders this time, I shinnied up the rope as simply as climbing a flight of stairs.

Where was this a week ago?

I launched instantly into a workout—a 400-meter run, 5 rope climbs, and 50 push-ups. I breezed right through each of the rope climbs.

One weakness cured.

But there was another weakness the rope had revealed that no one else was seeing. I know not every person in the world saw my failure on the rope climb, although it sure felt that way. The other weakness, though, had been exposed only to me because it took place within me. And unlike with the rope, there would be no quick fix.

One and Done?

In the first few months after the Games, I struggled with doubts over whether I would even want to go back to compete in another Games. I still liked CrossFit, but I didn't like the idea of competing. When I thought of the work it would take to make it to a second Games, I felt intense pressure I had never experienced as an athlete. I've always been one of those athletes who gets nervous before competition—the butterflies fluttering in the gut. It was that way in baseball and football, and it's that way in CrossFit. But I had never really struggled with the type of nervousness that can lock up an athlete and hamper his performance. Instead, it was more of an anticipation and a buildup to a game or a competition.

This pressure was different, though. It was the type that comes from putting too much importance on a result or outcome. It was a pressure that said I *had* to do better than second place next time; I had to win. I'm not sure why I believed I had to win, but that's what I felt, and it was strong enough of a feeling to make me not want to compete.

Complicating matters was a back problem I couldn't shake.

I had been unhappy with my form and technique on deadlifts and made it a priority to fix them. I was at a seminar at CrossFit Atlanta in August, and we were doing max deadlifts when I felt something kind of let go in my lower back. I didn't hurt right away, but when I got out of my car after the four-hour drive home from Georgia, I almost doubled over from an excruciating pain. It was miserable, like the worst kind of pulled muscle imaginable.

My back hurt when I lay down. It hurt when I stood up. It hurt when I sat. Anytime I picked up something from the ground, the pain would shoot in all directions. Squatting hurt. I couldn't find a way to loosen my back muscles. I was unable to lift anything, and working out was practically impossible.

I made several visits to a doctor and a chiropractor, but they couldn't identify the cause of the pain. The doctor, though, did give me prescriptions for a steroid pack, an anti-inflammatory medicine, and a painkiller. I left the doctor after that visit with no known reason for my back problem but a lot of prescriptions anyway. I remember thinking, *No wonder we have a drug problem in America!* I didn't take any of the medicine.

After three months of frustration with my back, I reached out to Kelly Starrett, a CrossFit gym owner in San Francisco, through his MobilityWOD.com website. Kelly has a doctorate in physical therapy, and I consider him a muscles guru.

I described my situation to Kelly, and he suggested exercises such as the couch stretch and others to help with the mobility of my hips and psoas muscles. The couch stretch basically involves kneeling on the floor (or a couch) as close to the wall as you can get, with the bottom part of your leg up against the wall (or the back of the couch). You lean forward, then back, really stretching the quads and psoas muscles in a way that hurts at first but soon begins to help loosen things up. My back began to improve immediately after starting the exercises, and within a couple of weeks it had healed enough that I could begin returning to my customary workouts.

The odd thing is that there had been moments when I wondered if I would ever be able to lift weights again because of my back, but my injury actually turned out to be insignificant. I just wasn't able to get it taken care of because I didn't know the proper stretches for that part of my back.

We were into December by that point, and although I work out year-round with multiple workouts almost every day, January was when I began to ramp up in preparation for the Games. But my knees were hurting like they were flaring up with tendinitis. I'd had to alter my squat to compensate for my back, and my knees were paying the price.

The workouts weren't fun when I was going through them in Games mode. In the middle of a workout, I'd think, *This is stupid. I don't want to do this.* After a workout, I'd notice that I felt better physically than before the workout, but at the same time I would already be dreading the workout later that day or the next morning. I felt mentally ruined from a competition standpoint. The only way I could get myself to work out was to not set specific times or reps as goals. Even though that kept me working out, I had no interest in competing again.

I didn't feel right physically. Mentally I was unsure of what I wanted to do. But I would soon come to realize that the weakness I needed to correct more than any other was spiritual.

Asking Questions

In January, I took a job as assistant strength coach at Tennessee Tech, working with athletes from all the sports teams but specifically from the baseball team. I was excited to be employed at my alma mater and especially as a strength coach. I had started studying for a master's degree, and with Darren's and my CrossFit gym going, I viewed the position as a good career move. I couldn't know then how great of a *life* move that job would prove to be.

The person who hired me was Chip Pugh, my teacher from the Training for Performance class who had sparked my interest in CrossFit. Chip also was the one who had raised the possibility of one day hiring me to work with him in the Tech athletic department or at his CrossFit affiliate.

Chip invited me to take part in a CrossFit-related organization he had started called CrossFit Faith. CrossFit Faith wasn't a gym but a group. Chip, who is also a minister, provided group members with a "spiritual WOD," such as a Scripture to memorize or a passage to read followed by questions to reflect on.

CrossFit Faith put me in close contact with a group of solid believers. There were guys in the group whom I had hung out with and I knew had been involved in campus ministries, but even though we were friends, none of their involvement in ministries had previously interested me.

During college, I had begun to drift spiritually. I stopped attending church regularly. If my girlfriend at the time went to church, I'd go with her, but without what I considered a home church, I didn't go on my own. I had read the Bible regularly through high school, and while the frequency of my reading had dropped off in college, I still did read it often. But all my motivation had come from needing something from God.

During rough patches in my life, I'd typically pull out my Bible, read some Scriptures, and ask God for what I needed. I wasn't truly studying the Bible. I'm not one to settle for "good enough," but that was what I had done spiritually. Reading Scripture when I needed to—not studying it consistently—had become good enough for me. Not surprisingly, the life I was leading wasn't feeling good enough for me.

Changes began to occur when I joined CrossFit Faith, and a big reason was that I was spending more time with believers like Chip and Thomas Cox, an assistant football coach. The more time I spent with those guys, the more impressed I became with how they lived out the spiritual principles they talked about. They were strong in their faith and they were passionate about it, and it was obvious that their faith was making a difference in their lives. What I observed in Chip and Thomas and other members of the group was different from what I was accustomed to seeing. What they were getting out of their time in God's Word obviously had effects in their lives that it wasn't having in mine.

That made me curious, and my curiosity led me to begin studying my Bible myself instead of merely reading it when I needed a favor from God. I started with Matthew, and right away, I gained an appreciation for the life Jesus led and the sacrifice He made on the cross so that we—I—could have eternal salvation through Him. I had been reading God's Word for pretty much all my life, but when I began studying consistently with CrossFit Faith and on my own, Scripture took on an entirely new meaning. I've heard people express how the Bible "came alive" to them, and that's the way it was for me. The stories I had been reading for all those years were no longer just isolated events. They flowed together as part of a bigger story. For the first time in my life, I really understood the Bible—not just the words I was reading, but everything that the Bible was. Where I had only been scratching the surface of Scripture before, I now was digging to go as deep as I could.

It was during this time of newfound excitement over

opening the Bible each day that Chip asked me the question for which I did not have an answer: "Why do you do what you do?" And when Donovan started our conversation during the car ride home from the seminar, that prompted me to analyze my view of God.

Those all combined to cause me to enter the deepest period of self-reflection of my life. I knew I had to find the answers to those questions.

What is my purpose in life?
Why am I here?
Why do I do CrossFit?
Who am I?
What am I?

CHAPTER 11

SIGNIFICANT LOSSES

MEME, MY GRANDMOTHER on my dad's side, had a significant spiritual influence on my life as I grew up. To me, Meme was the perfect example of a life well lived, and I look back now with regret over not having had more serious talks with her, particularly about faith. Even today, I find myself wishing I could sit down with her and share my excitement over my Bible studies and ask questions to draw on her spiritual experience.

Meme passed away between when I quit college baseball and when I began working for the fire department to get back into school. I was nineteen then, young and immature. I thought I had it all together.

Meme was short, and her reddish hair was short too. When my sister and I slept over at Meme and Papa's, whether in Michigan or in their trailer when they came to visit us in Cookeville, Meme wore those long nightgowns that must have been made for only grandmothers to wear.

She loved tulips, but she had lupus and had to be careful not to spend too much time in sunlight. She would put on her big gardening hat to block the sun and stay outside as long as she could to take care of her prized tulips.

Meme told me one time about how my birth had brought a type of healing for her. My aunt—my dad's younger sister—had died about a year before I was born, and it devastated my grandma. The pain she described feeling for that year made it sound like my aunt's death absolutely crushed her. Her faith got rocked, and she asked a lot of *why* questions. But my birth, Meme told me, helped bring her out of her dark place.

My sister, Kayla, and I were our grandparents' only grandkids, and we were appropriately spoiled by them. When we stayed with them in Michigan, one of our favorite things to do was go to the Detroit Zoo. The hippopotamus was my favorite animal . . . until our first zoo trip, when I smelled the hippos and their hippo house. After that I changed my favorite animal to the tiger in honor of the Detroit Tigers.

When Kayla and I were young, Meme would record herself reading stories and mail the cassette tapes to us. A package from Meme would arrive about every three or four months, and we would get so excited at the chance to find out which stories she had selected for us that we'd start playing them as soon as we opened the package. In the days and weeks that followed, we'd keep listening to the stories. Sometimes Kayla and I would listen to Meme's stories together, but most of the time we would take a cassette each into our rooms and listen alone to her reading to us.

Some of the stories were the typical children's bedtime stories and others were Christian stories for kids. Every one had an underlying meaning about life or faith that she wanted us to pick up on.

I still can recall hearing her clock chiming in the background in the room where she recorded the stories. I would count the chimes so I could know what time it had been when Meme had read to us. Knowing the time was one more connection I could make to her.

As I listened to her read, I could do more than hear her voice. I also could feel her hugs because Meme was a big hugger. Hello, good-bye, good morning, good afternoon, good job—all were enough of a reason for my grandma to give someone a hug.

Meme loved life. My dad, my cousin Donnie, and I got kicks out of making her laugh. (Though Donnie was a cousin on my mom's side, Meme always treated him like her own grandson.) Typical of our competitive nature, we liked to see who could draw the biggest laugh out of Meme. For some reason, *Forrest Gump* quotes were a surefire way to get a laugh from her. And her laugh was contagious. When Meme thought something was funny, everyone else in the room laughed too.

Meme made a big deal out of holidays, but Easter was her favorite. She would decorate her house to a T for Easter. She included Easter eggs, but religious themes made up most of the decorations. I can still see the images of Jesus and lambs all around her house during the Easter season.

To me, with the spiritual state of my life then, Christmas was the big holiday. Our family intentionally kept Christ in our Christmases, but the receiving of gifts was the most important part of Christmas for me. I understand now why Easter was Meme's favorite holiday—she really got it. She completely grasped the significance of remembering Christ's resurrection from the grave.

I've said how our grandparents would come to Cookeville and stay in a trailer on our property. They also talked a great deal about looking forward to the day when Papa would retire from GM and they could move to Tennessee permanently to be near us. During the time I was working on the factory assembly line, my grandpa was very close to retiring, and they had picked out a place in Crossville, about forty miles southeast of Cookeville, where they would build their retirement home.

Meme came to Tennessee to finish up plans on the house while Papa stayed back home to work, and she started running a fever and having aches and chills, along with vomiting. We assumed she had the flu, but when the symptoms didn't go away after a few days, she went to a local hospital. Doctors discovered that Meme had suffered a heart attack.

Talk about a shock to us all.

Meme was transferred to Vanderbilt University Medical Center in Nashville. Over the next three or four days, she would get better, then worse. Then she would get better and then worse again. It was an emotional roller coaster for the entire family. On November 22, 2005—a date I've never forgotten—she passed away in the hospital.

That was a tough time. I think I handled her death well, but I dealt with serious grief for a couple of months. At least I knew that because Meme had been strong in her faith, she had gone to heaven. But still, I missed my grandma and the spiritual influence she had on me.

After Meme's death was when I went through the stage where I began to attend church less and have a distant, self-serving relationship with God. I don't think that happened because Meme died, but I do wonder if my spiritual condition might have been different if she and Papa had moved to Tennessee and I had been around her more. Who knows? As I grew older, perhaps Meme and I might have had those grown-up conversations I hadn't known I needed to have with her.

When "Next Time" Doesn't Come

A year before Meme passed away, I experienced for the first time the pain of losing a family member. It was February 10, 2004, during my junior year in high school. I was watching our school's basketball team play a game. Basketball was never my sport, so I was content to sit in the stands and watch my friends play.

During the game that night, one of our school's coaches motioned for me to come down out of the stands and told me, "You need to get home."

"Okay," I said, not sure what else to say.

I had no idea what to expect when I got there, but I thought it was probably good news that I was told to go home. If something really bad had happened to one of my parents, I figured I would have been directed to the hospital.

When I walked through the door, my mom was bawling hysterically.

"What's wrong?" I asked.

"Matt" was all she said.

"Matt who?"

"Your cousin. He's passed away."

My mom's sister, Aunt Chris, had six sons: Donnie, Mitchell, Dustin, Marcus, Darren, and Matt.

Mom said she didn't know much other than that Matt had died from a gunshot wound.

After barely sleeping, Mom, my sister, and I set out early the next morning on the ten-hour drive to Michigan. On the many trips we had made back home, especially when I was a youngster, that drive seemed hopelessly long because I was eager to see all our family again, especially the cousins. But on none of those trips had the drive seemed as long as that one. I had plenty of time to think about Matt.

All of us cousins loved the outdoors, but Matt was a true outdoorsman. Sometimes I think he lived to hunt and fish. I couldn't get out of my mind the last time we had been to

Michigan. Matt had wanted me to go hunting with him, but I didn't because I had other things I wanted to do with Donnie, his oldest brother, who was the closest cousin to my age.

"Next trip," I told Matt.

Now, that next trip was for Matt's funeral.

I reflected on the fun times with Matt.

One time, Matt took me raccoon hunting. We were out in the woods, and he asked me, "You see that raccoon up in that tree?"

I couldn't. All I could see was a hole in the tree. "What are you talking about?" I asked.

Matt answered by raising his gun, taking aim at the hole, and firing. A raccoon fell out of the hole.

"How did you see that?" I asked him.

Matt kept pointing out spots where he could see raccoons—and I couldn't—and kept shooting those raccoons.

Matt could have easily lived in the woods. He was adventurous outdoors from an early age.

One winter, when Matt was about five, there was a family of Canada geese that had made a home at Uncle Don and Aunt Chris's pond. Matt took off running toward the geese and grabbed one of the goslings, then dashed off in the other direction. The adult geese began hot pursuit of Matt and the kidnapped gosling, but Matt just kept running.

We half laughed and half tried to convince Matt to turn the gosling loose, but he was having too much fun being chased to let go. The chase went on for several minutes, with

Matt running and laughing and those riled-up adult geese squawking at him the entire time. Finally Matt turned back toward the pond and on his way past tossed the gosling into the water. The young goose came back above the surface, and other than looking a little confused about the past five minutes of his life, acted fine. With the gosling safe and okay, the adult geese called off their chase.

When Matt was a little older—six, I think—we were fishing and Matt grabbed at what he thought was a frog. But what he pulled out of the water actually was a snapping turtle. Matt was as surprised as we were, but he kept his grip on the turtle's head as it kept trying to bite at his hand.

"What are you doing?" we asked him.

"Big frog!" was all he said, then burst out in laughter.

That was Matt—living wide open and fearless.

As much as Matt loved life, he also faced a few challenges. He had ADD, and his family and doctors had been working to find the right way to regulate it with medicine. Matt's mind was always going full speed, and he was always wanting to do some type of activity. That got him into trouble in school occasionally. It wasn't major trouble because Matt wasn't a trouble-maker, but he was reprimanded for things like talking in class when he wasn't supposed to or being too loud.

Matt did have one fear: sleeping alone in the dark. Because of Matt's fear, on one of my summer visits, I slept in Matt's room when I stayed at his house. We stayed up late and joked around, but we also had some good talks. That was the summer I grew close to Matt.

Arm wrestling with my dad

Reading with Meme

See? I *can* climb!

Playing for Cookeville High School

I loved the time I spent working with the Cookeville Fire Department. I learned a lot about myself and developed a lifelong respect and admiration for the men and women who put their lives on the line every day to help save others.

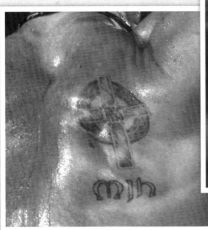

Tattoo tribute for Matt

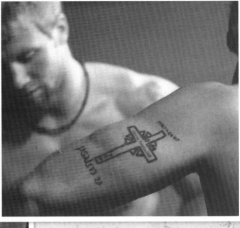

Tattoo tribute for Donnie

MJH and DGH: they are with me at every competition.

"In Loving Memory of Donnie & Matt Hunsucker": they were with me on my wedding day too.

◀ Proposing to Hillary at the exact spot where her parents were married

Hillary is awesome. She watches and cheers for me, but she really doesn't care if I finish first, second, or dead last. She's perfect for me because she keeps balance in my life. I could easily overload on CrossFit if it weren't for her keeping me in check.

With my sister, Kayla

With my mom and dad
on my wedding day

With Darren, my cousin,
business partner, workout
partner, and best man (not to
mention the guy who lost my
wedding ring)

Hillary, meet Dan. He's going to
be living with us for . . . a while.

◀ 95-pound squat snatch at Sectionals in Huntsville, Alabama

THE 2010 GAMES

▲ Pull-ups—no problem

▲ 135-pound squat snatch—no problem

Muscle-ups—no problem

Rope climb—small problem

Dog Sled—pushing a
465-pound sled 40 feet

GHD sit-ups, part of a four-round triplet

Traveling 100 feet on the monkey bars—
just one element of the Killer Kage

The final event of the Games: pulling a
465-pound sled 78 feet

Coming out of the water
during the triathlon

Sled Push—20 yards,
five rounds

THE 2012 GAMES

◄ Working my way up
the clean ladder with a
335-pound lift

Running the last element ►
of the track triplet—the
400-meter sprint

2-TIME CHAMPION

◀ Muscle-ups in my garage

135-pound thrusters ▶

◀ Box-jumps

Rowing ▶

◀ With
my loyal
training
buddy,
Gilligan

Taking a short
breather
▼

"But far be it from me to boast except in the cross of our Lord Jesus Christ, by which the world has been crucified to me, and I to the world."

GALATIANS 6:14

Now, just a few years later, Matt was unexpectedly gone. He was fourteen years old.

When we arrived at his family's home, I went downstairs to the basement because that's where the cousins had always hung out. There were people cleaning out the room where the shotgun had accidentally gone off.

Matt was a good kid from a good family, and he had a big heart and loved to have fun. Then, out of seemingly nowhere, his life had ended.

Losing My Best Friend

Donnie was the oldest brother in the Hunsucker family. He also was the cousin I was closest to growing up. Although we were born only twelve days apart, Donnie was older than me, and he liked to rub that fact in my face. In all the competitiveness that took place among the cousins, Donnie was the one I was most competitive with.

Donnie was my best friend, and after Matt's death, he and I grew even closer. For one thing, Matt's death made me realize for the first time just how short life could be. I didn't know when I told Matt that I'd go hunting with him next time that I would never have that opportunity. Matt's death taught me that our "next times" are not guaranteed. As a result, I spent more time calling, e-mailing, and texting my cousins—Donnie especially.

Frankly Donnie needed me because he really took Matt's death hard. Donnie embraced the honor and responsibility of being a big brother, and he was a great big brother. With the Hunsucker boys, it was the old case of "We can pick on each other, but no one outside of our family can pick on any of us." There wasn't much of a limit on what those boys would do to one another, but Donnie was the chief protector of his younger brothers against anyone outside the family. When Matt died, Donnie struggled with the idea that he should have done more to protect him. Of course, there wasn't anything more he could have done, but that's not the way you think when you've gone through a traumatic situation like Donnie and his family.

Making matters worse for Donnie was the final time he and Matt had spoken. The night we arrived in Michigan for Matt's funeral, Donnie and I talked in the basement room next to where Matt had been shot. Donnie recounted how he'd found out that Matt had gotten into minor trouble at school for being mischievous, and he and Matt met up in the lunchroom the day of Matt's death. Matt sent a little smirk in Donnie's direction.

"Don't smile at me," Donnie told Matt. "You know what you did."

Those were the last words Donnie spoke to his brother.

They were harmless words, but in the aftermath of what had happened in the room next to us, Donnie regretted them.

Raw pain covered Donnie's face and was clear in his voice as he shared that story with me. From then on, even though I really didn't want to, I tried to imagine what kept running through Donnie's mind in the weeks and months after Matt's accident.

After Matt passed away, I decided to get my first tattoo as a way of honoring him. It's on my right shoulder blade, and because of our family's Irish-Catholic heritage, I got a Celtic cross with Matt's initials—*MJH*—in Celtic lettering below the cross. Inside the cross are the letters *IHS* for *In His Service*. Donnie loved the tattoo.

Our family has a tendency to show up unannounced for weekends or family members' birthdays, even if they're a ten-hour drive away. It wouldn't be too out of the ordinary for the doorbell to ring and ten members of our family from Michigan to be standing at the front door with suitcases in hand.

Donnie made one of those trips with his family to see us for Mom's birthday in 2006. Once he was there, he decided to stay for a whole week. My mom had planned on going to Michigan that week, so Donnie and I had full run of the apartment Mom was living in. We were good boys for the most part, and the only major trouble came when Donnie returned home. With just the two of us to watch out for each other, Donnie had decided that he wanted a tattoo like mine. Even though the tattoo honored his brother, his parents were less than thrilled when Donnie showed up with a tattoo.

There was one other event that almost happened that week that would have been a bigger development than Donnie getting a tattoo.

We came *this* close to enlisting in the Navy.

Donnie and I went through a stage where we wanted to become Navy SEALs. We had it all figured out. We would sign up together, go through training together, and then become SEALs together. Our research had alerted us to the high dropout rate of would-be SEALs, but we were convinced that if we were in training together, we would be able to push each other through the process. With the other one there, we were certain neither of us would give up.

Confident in our plan, we talked to a Navy recruiter two or three times and wound up in his office to sign the papers to enlist. The recruiter was going through all the necessary questions with us, and we were getting close to the end, when it would be time to officially sign up.

"Have either of you had any surgeries?" the recruiter asked.

"I had shoulder surgery," I answered.

"When was that?" he asked.

"After my junior year of high school."

"No big deal," he said and resumed his path down the list. "Have either of you ever had seizures?" he asked.

Potential problem.

Donnie had suffered three or four seizures that I knew of. He wasn't epileptic, but he apparently was prone to seizures when sleep deprived. Anyone who knows about BUD/S training for SEALs is aware that during Hell Week, SEAL candidates get only a handful of hours of sleep over five days because being able to carry out missions while sleep deprived is an essential requirement of being a SEAL.

"I've had a few," Donnie replied.

"Ah, don't worry about it—you'll be fine," the recruiter told him.

"Hold on a minute," I interrupted.

I instantly thought of the possibility that a sleep-deprived Donnie could have a seizure that would get him booted out of SEAL training. Then I'd be left to go at it alone. I wasn't that confident in my ability to complete the training process without Donnie there. And then Donnie would get some kind of job like being a cook on a ship in the middle of the ocean instead of being a SEAL like he wanted, and who knew where I would wind up. I figured odds were slim that Donnie and I would be together.

We didn't give the recruiter an opportunity to skirt around any more potential legitimate issues; we got out of that office, leaving our SEAL dreams behind.

Donnie was supposed to have caught a ride back to Michigan with another cousin who had come through Tennessee on his way home from spring break in Florida, but because of our grand plans of joining the Navy, we'd told our cousin to continue home alone. That left Donnie without a way home. Donnie's dad had to use frequent flyer miles to get Donnie a flight to Michigan.

I remember walking with Donnie through the airport. He hadn't brought any luggage of his own when his family drove down, so the "suitcase" he carried as we said good-bye was a Rubbermaid container that we had duct-taped shut. It had been a most excellent week together.

Donnie and I stayed in touch with each other after that, but life got in the way for both of us, and we weren't in contact as much as before. He was in college, and I was in college, and the number of our trips to see each other dropped off.

I still feel guilty about that, because on December 30, 2007, Mom got another horrible phone call from Michigan.

She came downstairs that morning, crying loudly again.

Donnie, she told me, had been killed in a car accident.

Donnie, who was twenty, had been at a friend's house late on a Saturday and into early Sunday morning. Donnie was tired, and his friend suggested he spend the night at his house, but Donnie said he had promised his mom that he would go to church with the family the next morning.

At 3 a.m., and just a few minutes from home, Donnie apparently fell asleep at the wheel. His car slammed into a tree, driver's-side door first, and Donnie died instantly.

Just as we had almost four years earlier, we made another long drive for a cousin's funeral.

They say no one should have to go through the experience of burying a child, but Uncle Don and Aunt Chris were about to bury a second child. Yet Aunt Chris came up to me and asked, "Are you okay?"

I couldn't believe that with everything she had gone through with Matt and was going through again with Donnie, she was that concerned about me. I'll never forget the strong faith she displayed during her time of loss.

My cousin Rachel is also real close to my age. It had always been the three of us—Donnie, Rachel, and me—who usually found a way to group together because of our ages. When we were with the family in Michigan and I saw Rachel, it hit me hard that one of us was gone. There would never again be the three of us.

Donnie's funeral was big. We were told that more than a thousand people attended. Several people got up to speak, and there were a lot of great things said about Donnie. He was such a wonderful, respected, well-loved person. There were many people at that funeral whom Donnie had made feel like his best friend, but I knew beyond doubt that Donnie was my best friend. I had things I wanted to say about him, but I had a fear of public speaking, so I didn't say anything. I've regretted that since.

We visited the site of Donnie's crash. It was eerie because there was only one tree in that field where his car left the road. One tree, and Donnie's car struck it. From looking at the tree, we could tell how violent the impact had been. The driver's-side seat had been slammed into the passenger's seat.

I sliced a small piece of bark from the tree as a keepsake to remember Donnie. The tree was later cut down, and part of it was used to make a rocking chair for his dad, my uncle Don. I hung my piece of bark from the mirror in my bedroom so I would see it every day. I took it down after a couple of years. The memories of Donnie that the bark kept fresh in my mind were good for me, but at the same time its presence stirred up more pain than I wanted to face.

Defining a Legacy

Even after Donnie's death, and Meme's before his, and Matt's before hers, I never became angry with God. But I did begin to ask myself questions about why I was still here when they weren't. Why I had been allowed to keep living when they hadn't.

Then, in the time after the 2010 Games, when Chip Pugh and Donovan Degrie asked me questions about my purpose in life, six years' worth of events rolled up together to create one question.

If I die, what legacy am I going to leave?

I kept pondering the question.

If I die, what legacy am I going to leave?

I didn't like the answer I came up with.

CrossFit.

CrossFit would be my legacy?

Not even a year earlier, few outside of my friends and family had reason to know who I was. But because of my success in CrossFit competitions, I now had become known as Rich Froning the CrossFitter. I understood that. Finishing second at the Games had brought attention to me through numerous interviews, and the interviewers wanted to know about my barn-to-Games story, about my multiple workouts per day, about my atypical diet plan, about my thoughts on coming back to try to win the 2011 Games. The interviews all centered around CrossFit, so how else were people who didn't know me supposed to look at me, other than as a CrossFitter?

The problem was that I had begun to identify myself as a CrossFitter.

As someone who coaches people in CrossFit, I've observed with interest the role that purpose plays in CrossFit. I'm talking about regular people—the people CrossFit was created for, not the athletes competing on TV. The workouts are difficult, so one of the first things we determine with people who are new to our gym is their purpose for starting CrossFit. They must have an end goal, or experience has taught us that they won't stick with it. I've seen that countless times. I've also experienced that in my workouts. When I started working out, I wanted to be fitter. Then, when I started competing—even when Darren and I were in the barn comparing our numbers to others' online—I wanted to become one second faster. To lift 5 pounds more. To complete one more rep.

But I had gone to an extreme and allowed CrossFit to become my purpose. I had allowed it to take over who I was. I had become, in my own mind as well as in the minds of others, Rich Froning the CrossFitter.

It wasn't a case of success going to my head. The people around me would not have allowed that to happen. Trust me, my family and close friends have a way of keeping me humble. It wasn't all about the competitions, either. For a few months after the 2010 Games, my back was really bothering me, and I wasn't sure I'd be able to compete in 2011. I wasn't even sure I really *wanted* to compete again. But I did know that I was going to stick with CrossFit.

I still enjoyed working out, and Darren and I had our gym up and running.

I just could not get away from the sense that I was meant to have a greater purpose in life than competing and coaching in CrossFit. I realized that if I were to die, people who didn't know me or knew little about me would remember me only for CrossFit. What really scared me, though, was the thought that if I were to die, even my own family—the people who knew me best and loved me most—might remember me more for CrossFit than anything else.

That was not the legacy I wanted to leave, and I determined to begin correcting that immediately.

That's where the emphasis on Bible study kicked in. I set out to study the Gospels, starting with Matthew. After the Gospels, I kept on going right through the rest of the New Testament.

One thing I noticed almost instantly about studying God's Word was my desire to not only share what I was learning with others but also to be around others who would share with me what they were learning in their studies.

Hillary was more spiritually mature than me. We began studying the Bible and praying together every night and, as a result, grew closer to God and to each other.

My relationship with God strengthened, and my relationship with Hillary strengthened. It was like the illustration of the triangle I've seen numerous times concerning dating and marriage relationships. The speaker would write the man's name at one of the corners on the base of the triangle and the woman's name at the other. Then he would write God's name at the top of the triangle and point out that as the man and the woman both grew closer to God, they also grew closer to each other.

It was true.

CHAPTER 12

FINDING PEACE

The change in venue from 2009 to 2010 had marked a significant transition for the CrossFit Games. Two additional major changes in 2011 pushed CrossFit further into the mainstream: Reebok signed on as the Games' title sponsor, and the renamed Reebok CrossFit Games would be broadcast on ESPN2 for the first time.

Reebok's sponsorship boosted the total purse to $1 million, including $250,000 going to both the men's and women's winners. By comparison, Graham Holmberg had received $25,000 for winning the 2010 Games. (The first Games winners had received $500; that increased to $1,500 in 2008 and $5,000 the next year.) As runner-up in 2010,

I had received a $500 gift card from Under Armour. Two months later, I signed an endorsement contract with Reebok, so that took care of wearing any Under Armour purchases.

The Games had previously been aired live online through ESPN3, but having the Games edited and packaged to be broadcast on ESPN2 about a month and a half later was guaranteed to raise interest in the sport and, more important, cause more people to become interested in improving their lifestyles through CrossFit.

CrossFit was already exploding, and that led to a substantial format change for 2011.

The Sectionals round was replaced by what was called the Open round of qualifying. The CrossFit Open basically opened up the competition to anyone who wanted to give it a try. Instead of requiring competitors to attend a Sectional competition, such as the one I had traveled to in Alabama the year before, Open qualifying would take place either through local CrossFit affiliates or through individual videos posted online.

The Open consisted of five weekly workouts, beginning in March. Each week's workout was posted online on Tuesday. Anyone who wanted to do the workout could; athletes had until the following Sunday to perform the workout at a local CrossFit affiliate and have their performance verified. Alternately, they could video the workout and submit the result online for the CrossFit community to judge.

The cost to take part in the Open was only ten dollars in the United States and Canada and five dollars in all other countries. As a result, anyone with a few bucks and a way to record the workout could try to qualify for Regionals. The top sixty Open qualifiers from each of the seventeen regions worldwide would advance.

The new format came partly because of logistical problems with trying to hold enough Sectionals to meet the demands of the surging number of competitors, but it also served two other main purposes: it maximized participation and was the best way to truly determine the Fittest on Earth.

The Open probably really was the best way possible of realistically eliminating geographic and financial limitations. This way, some guy in Bulgaria or Chile or the Philippines— as long as he had a flip phone and the equivalent of five US dollars—wouldn't be able to watch the 2011 Games and say he actually was the Fittest Man on Earth but hadn't been given the opportunity to prove it.

The participation numbers were astounding, as more than 26,000 people took part in the 2011 CrossFit Open.

By virtue of my second-place finish at the 2010 Games, I didn't have to go through qualifying in the Open or at Regionals in 2011. I did, though, take part in the team competition of the Central East Regional—Tennessee's region in the new geographic alignment—so I could try to help my workout partners from CrossFit Faith qualify for the team portion of the Games. We didn't qualify, finishing eighth, but participating gave me the opportunity to go through the atmosphere of Regionals with the safety net of already having secured a spot in the Games.

A Permanent Message

For me, personally, that time during the 2011 Open workouts was when the remaining loose ends began to come together. Through my Bible study and prayer time, I found the answer to Chip's question, "Why do you do what you do?"

I determined that my purpose was to bring glory to God in everything I do. CrossFit, I concluded, would no longer be about me, but a very public way I could go about glorifying God.

My friend Donovan had been kicking around the idea of getting a tattoo with the verse Galatians 2:20: "I have been crucified with Christ. It is no longer I who live, but Christ who lives in me. And the life I now live in the flesh I live by faith in the Son of God, who loved me and gave himself for me."

I told Donovan I thought the tattoo would be a good idea because of the verse's message.

"There's another verse you need to look at," Donovan suggested.

"Which one?" I asked.

"Galatians 6:14," he said.

I looked up the verse.

"But far be it from me to boast except in the cross of our Lord Jesus Christ, by which the world has been crucified to me, and I to the world."

That's it! I thought. *That's my verse.*

That verse perfectly described how I had come to view CrossFit and how I wanted others to view me through

CrossFit. I didn't want any glory that people might send my way because of my accomplishments in the Games. Instead, I wanted everything I did and said to be a reflection of God, to be a public recognition that my talents and abilities were given to me by Him. Because without God, I would not have been able to do any of the things I had done in CrossFit. I had absolutely nothing to brag about—it was all what God had done through me for a purpose He had designed for me.

I liked the verse so much that I decided I wanted to get it as a tattoo. I already had two tattoos. The first was the one on my shoulder blade that included Matt's initials. The second, which I had gotten three months after Donnie's accident, was on my right triceps and was one I had designed myself: the firefighters' Maltese cross set behind a representation of Christ's cross. Inside that cross, I had my cousin Donnie's name and my grandma Meme's initials inscribed. Above the cross were the dates of Donnie's life, *1987–2007*, and below it was *Psalm 23*, which was read at Donnie's and Meme's funerals.

I decided to get *Galatians 6:14* tattooed on my right side, running up under my arm and toward my shoulder. I'm not sure why I chose that particular spot, but I was glad I did because it was a place where the verse stood out while I did many of the CrossFit movements.

The tattoo also was easily visible to me, and it instantly began serving as both a declaration and a reminder of my purpose, of why I am here. I hadn't considered that the tattoo would be a form of accountability, but that's what it has turned out to be. I'm always self-evaluating, asking if I'm doing what I need to be doing, living what I'm preaching, and being a good example. The tattoo has become a good self-check for me.

Mr. and Mrs. Froning

Two momentous events took place between Regionals and the Games.

First, in May, I was baptized by Chip. I had been baptized as a three-month-old in our Catholic church in Michigan, but as I studied the New Testament and came across passages that included baptism, I wondered whether mine had "counted." Baptism is a public profession of faith, and I didn't see how as a three-month-old, I could have been old enough to make a public profession of anything other than being hungry or needing a diaper change.

I asked Chip about it because he was a minister.

"You know," he said, "that's pretty cool that you thought about it."

I thought some of my Catholic family might not like me getting baptized again, but as I prayed about it, in my heart it kept feeling like the right thing for me to do. I wanted to get baptized, and so did Hillary's mom, Patty. Chip baptized both of us in the Caney Fork River at Rock Island State Park with our families and close friends watching.

Then, on June 18, 2011, almost six weeks before the Games, Hillary and I married under the same chestnut trees where her parents had married. My friend Bret Ellis conducted the ceremony. Bret, who owns CrossFit Rabid in Rainbow City, Alabama, had been one of my judges at the 2010 Sectionals. We became close friends, and Bret has helped me as an athlete, as a coach, and spiritually.

Admittedly, the timing of our wedding probably wasn't the best as far as training for the Games was concerned, but we had gotten engaged back in April 2010. At that time, we had no way of knowing all the changes that would take place over the following fourteen months—that I would make it to the 2010 Games, much less finish second, and that I would go into 2011 labeled as one of the top contenders for the title of Fittest Man on Earth.

Four months before the big day, Dad told me, "You need to talk to Hillary about postponing the wedding."

I just looked at him for a second before saying, "*You* need to talk to Hillary about postponing the wedding."

Dad knew better than to incur the wrath of Hillary, so the idea of moving back our wedding date advanced no further.

The big issue Hillary and I had to settle was whether to go on a honeymoon right after the wedding or wait until after the Games, the last weekend of July.

Because I had been slowed by the back injury and the uncertainty in my mind about competing in 2011, I still had a lot of catching up to do to prepare for the Games. Those weeks leading up to the Games would be my most intense training. I wouldn't be taking a day off.

Hillary understood how important the workouts would

be for me that close to the Games, and I understood that working out three or four times per day on our honeymoon was out of the question. So we came up with a compromise. We decided to take an abbreviated two-day honeymoon to Charleston, South Carolina. I would work out once each day (plus a workout the morning of the wedding). Then we would take a longer honeymoon immediately following the Games.

We had a big wedding, at least as far as attendants go. I had nine groomsmen—with as many cousins as I have, finding nine was easy—and we also listed three best men in the wedding party: my cousin and business/workout partner Darren, my friend Matt Billings, and Donnie.

After Donnie's accident, a group of us had rubber wristbands made that read, *In Loving Memory of Donnie & Matt Hunsucker*. Our wedding album includes a photo of the groomsmen and me displaying our wristbands together. I missed Donnie and Matt a lot that day.

I missed Meme that day too. I wished Hillary had been able to meet my grandmother, because they have a lot in common. Like Hillary, Meme was a positive person whom others loved to be around. They would have enjoyed each other's company, and it would have been a blast to watch them together. Hillary might have beaten us all at getting the biggest laughs out of Meme, and she probably could have done so without quoting *Forrest Gump*. I knew Meme would have approved of my bride.

Meekness—Not Weakness

My spiritual growth between the 2010 and 2011 Games did nothing to diminish my competitive nature. As a lifelong sports fan, I've heard of professional athletes who became Christians during their careers and were criticized for turning "soft." I find it difficult to believe that would be the case. I'm sure there have been athletes who became Christians and then felt God leading them in a different direction. But for the most part, I think someone who labels an athlete as "soft" because he's a Christian is either looking for a reason to criticize the athlete's faith or is coming up with an easy but incorrect explanation for an athlete's decline in performance. Especially for an athlete who was at the top of his or her sport or game. It's difficult enough just to get to the top, and it's even more difficult to remain there.

I once read a phrase that has stuck with me: "Meek does not mean weak." Jesus said in His Sermon on the Mount that the meek would inherit the earth, and Jesus described Himself as meek and humble in Matthew 11:29. Jesus certainly wasn't weak. He became angry enough to clear out the money changers from the Temple (John 2:13-16). Jesus was passionate about the sanctity of God's house, and that passion moved Him to honor the Temple. Passion moves people to take action. I'm passionate about competing in the Games and glorifying God while doing so, and that moves me to give my absolute best effort every time.

So the deepening of my faith had no negative effect on my

competitiveness. I've also competed with enough Christians in CrossFit to know that hasn't been the case for them, either. I don't want to throw a blanket statement out there that could be used to judge anyone, because like I said, we don't know how God is leading other people. But in my case, with my newfound purpose of seeking to glorify God through CrossFit, how could I not go all out during competition?

Colossians 3:23 says, "Whatever you do, work heartily, as for the Lord and not for men." To me, that should motivate Christians to give their all—whether it's at the Games, in a gym busting their butts in a workout, competing in another sport, or working a desk job. The point is, whatever you do should be done for God's glory, not yours.

To Plan or Not to Plan?

I went into the 2011 Games fully determined to win, and I believed that my workout routine over the five or six months leading up to the Games had me well prepared.

Actually, I probably shouldn't say I had a workout "routine." I've justifiably picked up a reputation for not following routines in my workouts. That method began in the run-up to the '11 Games.

With my job at that time, working with athletes at Tennessee Tech, I sometimes trained alongside our football players to set an example for them to follow and for my benefit too. I also tested workouts because we were using CrossFit for the players. I squeezed in my workouts during breaks in my coaching schedule and between the graduate classes I was taking. Some days, I completed up to five full workouts.

I wish I had kept records of my workouts because I get asked about my "routine" quite often. I didn't have a coach (and still don't), so I created my own workouts. I went a lot by feel in setting my workouts. Some of that came from the period when I wasn't sure I wanted to keep competing. I still liked working out, but when I thought of what I would need to do in preparation for the Games, my workouts felt like work. It was like I was thinking dreadfully, *I've gotta get this done.* Planning out every set ahead of time probably would have pushed me more toward that work-instead-of-workouts mind-set I was trying to avoid.

There were certain areas where I knew I needed to train every day to improve, such as getting stronger at Olympic lifts and working on my squats form. At my first Games, I had been way too quad dominant, and that had caused knee pain. In addition, I had experienced how difficult the Games were from a stamina standpoint, so I also focused on becoming as efficient as possible to conserve as much energy as possible. But other than those specific areas, I'd show up at the gym, think about what I hadn't done in a couple of days, and then incorporate those movements into a workout.

Working out multiple times a day, I had various training partners I'd meet at the gym, and I sometimes liked to let them set our workouts. Having somebody else determining what we would do was a way for me to practice handling the unknowable at the Games.

/// CROSSFIT DEFINED /////////////////////////////////////

OLYMPIC LIFTS

Olympic lifts include moves like the jerk, the clean, and the snatch. Basically, they're the kinds of weight-lifting movements performed in the Olympic Games. Olympic lifts are part of many CrossFit workouts, and they're important in improving overall strength and fitness.

///

CHAPTER 13

THE GAMES AGAIN

I FELT READY WHEN I arrived in California for the 2011 CrossFit Games. Until I got on the bus early, *early* on Friday morning.

In typical fashion, the Games started off with an unexpected event. We were told at the pre-Games meeting that we wouldn't be competing at the Home Depot Center to begin with. Instead, the first event would be held at Santa Monica Pier. The workout would be a combination swim and beach run.

We boarded the buses at 4 a.m. Friday at the hotel, and I was a nervous wreck. It wasn't my typical precompetition nervousness, and to this day I still haven't been able to identify why I was so nervous.

It was dark on the bus as we made our predawn ride to Santa Monica. I pulled out my phone and tapped my Bible app. I started off randomly flipping through before settling at Jeremiah 29:11-13 (NIV): "'For I know the plans I have for you,' declares the LORD, 'plans to prosper you and not to harm you, plans to give you hope and a future. Then you will call on me and come and pray to me, and I will listen to you. You will seek me and find me when you seek me with all your heart.'" I read each word of those verses, although I knew them all well.

In May, Chip and I had attended a conference for strength coaches. One of our CrossFit Faith spiritual workouts during the trip was to memorize Jeremiah 29:11-13. I've never been good at memorization, whether it be a Bible verse or a school assignment. That's frustrating because I'd like to be better at reciting Scripture. I can remember most of a Scripture verse and definitely its meaning, but word-for-word memorization is a weakness I'm working on. However, Jeremiah 29:11-13 was one passage that had successfully stuck in my brain.

As I sat in my bus seat and reflected on that passage, I thought of how I did not know what the future held, but I did know that God had a plan for me. In fact, even if I did have a plan, it wouldn't have mattered anyway. All that mattered was God's plan and that I prayerfully pursue His will for my life. As much as I wanted to win the Games, it wouldn't be important whether I did or not, because God had a plan for me and would take care of me. I didn't have to win to glorify God—I could do that regardless of where I finished.

All right! I thought as I kept reading through those verses on my phone. *Whatever happens, I'm gonna be all right!*

I didn't expect the nerves to go away completely, but I could feel them beginning to calm to their normal, manageable level.

Just so that no one assumes this is a story about me being inspired by a Bible verse and then everything suddenly going exactly as I wanted, I didn't win the first event. In fact, the first event went terribly! I'm glad, too, because it provides me with a stronger testimony. The message of the Jeremiah passage isn't about getting what we want—which, for me in that case, would have been winning the first event. Instead, that passage is more about trusting God and following His plan regardless of what happens in our lives.

For sure, I had a lot to deal with after what happened in the beach event.

At Santa Monica Pier, after a sprint across the beach, we had a 210-meter ocean swim, a 1,500-meter soft-sand run, 50 chest-to-bar pull-ups, 100 hand-release push-ups, 200 air squats, and another 1,500-meter soft-sand run to the finish line.

If you have been to Tennessee, you probably noticed we don't have an abundance of soft-sand beaches. I've been consistent in expressing my disdain for running. I'm not terrible at running—it's just that I don't like it. I find no joy whatsoever in running.

I discovered in the first event how much I hate running in soft sand. The swim didn't present a problem, and actually the first run wasn't too bad either. But that second 1,500-meter run at the end of the event was miserable. Keep in mind, 1,500 meters is just about a football field short of a full mile. Before I was done, I was having to alternate jogging and walking in the sand. I wasn't concerned about being able to finish, but I knew I wasn't going to end up with a good time.

There was nothing left in the tank when I crossed the finish line, finishing way back in twenty-sixth place out of forty-nine competitors.

Well, I analyzed to myself, *this isn't good.*

From a competitive standpoint, starting so poorly created an immediate momentum challenge for me because I had none after the first event. As I've said, you don't have to be the best in everything to win the Games, but you can't bomb in an event. Finishing twenty-sixth bordered on qualifying as a bomb. I recognized that, by giving myself that big of a hill to climb after the first morning, I had handed myself quite a challenge.

My poor performance also presented a spiritual challenge. I had come to the Games with the number one goal of glorifying God, and then I had felt His calming presence on the bus ride. Yet here I was feeling almost buried in the middle of the pack barely thirty minutes into the competition.

Isn't that typical of what often happens in our spiritual lives? We can enjoy a momentous experience that takes us to a new high in our faith, and then we can be immediately confronted with adversity that challenges us. I've noticed that some people view those moments as trials, while others view them as proving grounds. It's all a matter of perspective.

For me, the beach event was a proving ground because it proved that my newfound level of faith was the real deal. The way I felt after that event was a complete 180 from how I would have responded the year before. Then, I likely would have been devastated if I had gotten off to such a poor start. Yet now I was okay. It wasn't that I was okay with being in twenty-sixth place. Far from it. There were twenty-five guys ahead of me, and I knew how much work it would take for me to rise in the standings. I allowed myself to consider the possibility that I might only be able to make it up to somewhere around fifteenth or sixteenth place by Sunday night. I distinctly remember thinking, *If I finish fifteenth or sixteenth, my CrossFit competing days might be over. But I'm okay with it.*

Surprisingly I was completely at peace with that possibility. Although I had hoped that God's plan for me would include a CrossFit championship, the truth was I did not know what He had in store for me. But I knew that He *did* have a plan for me and that there was a bigger picture going on in my life than what I could see at that moment.

/// CROSSFIT DEFINED //

AIR SQUAT

Often just called a "squat" (squatting down so the crease of your hip is below your knee, then standing back up), an air squat is performed without any weight other than your own body. A squat done with weight is either a front squat or a back squat. A front squat is performed while holding a barbell in front of your shoulders in rack position; a back squat is performed with a barbell resting on your shoulders behind the neck.

///

Climbing the Hill

After the women completed their opening event at the beach, we were bused directly to the Home Depot Center to await the second event. Unlike in 2010, we were told what each event would be about an hour beforehand.

Having experienced both methods, I still haven't decided whether I prefer to know the events ahead of time or not.

When I know what an event will be, I can look ahead to which movements might give me the most trouble and identify places where my strengths might allow me the opportunity to make up time or reps. So much strategy and so many small things go into completing a CrossFit workout. Sometimes it's helpful to plan the details ahead of time, like at what point you'll be able to stop to catch your breath. So in that regard, it is good to have advance notice of what you'll be doing.

On the other hand, I feel like I'm well prepared for the unknown (despite what happened with the rope in 2010). The unknown is a tough competitor. It's not a very forgiving one sometimes, but because of the challenge it brings, the unknown also can add an element of fun.

Fortunately I don't have to decide whether I prefer to

know ahead of time or not, because Dave Castro isn't going to ask for my preference!

The second event, we were told, would be a three-part skills test at the track-and-field venue: L-sit for maximum time, softball toss for distance, and handstand walk for distance.

Out at the L-sit, I noticed other guys not wearing shoes. I was. *Why aren't they?* I asked myself. It wasn't long before I found out.

The L-sit is a gymnastics move that requires you to hold on to low parallel bars (called parallettes) and lift yourself so your legs are parallel to the ground, forming an L. For our event, weight plates were placed under our feet, and we had to hold our pose for as long as we could before our abs gave out and our feet touched the plates.

What I didn't realize until too late was that those who weren't wearing shoes gave themselves an extra inch or two of clearance between their heels and the plates. When you're holding that pose and your abs, triceps, and hips are beginning to burn, that inch or two becomes huge. I know I could have used that little bit of extra space, because my time was forty seconds—not as good as I had hoped. I tied for eleventh.

Here we go again.

To illustrate how much of a difference that extra inch or two could have made, consider that I tied for eleventh at forty seconds. If I could have held on for only two more seconds before making contact with the plates, I would have tied for seventh place.

After one event and one movement of the second event,

I had already messed up twice. It's tough to make two mistakes and still hang around the top of the leaderboard at the Games.

The second skill was the softball throw, where we were given two chances to throw for longest distance within a narrow lane.

Competitors familiar with my baseball background told me that I would have a big advantage in the softball throw, but they were more confident in me than I was. I guess they didn't know that I had been a second baseman, meaning that I was used to making more of a quick, short-armed throw that was very different from a distance throw. Most of them also didn't know that I had undergone surgery on my throwing shoulder.

As I watched, more of the early competitors than I expected had trouble with the softball throw. When my turn came, I made a safe throw on my first attempt. Even so, I barely qualified, as the ball landed on one of the lines. But having one number in the book let me air it out on my second try, and my throw of 229 feet, 10 inches was fourth best. The event was won by Spencer Hendel with a throw of 258 feet, 9 inches. Spencer also had been a high school baseball player, and he had undergone Tommy John ligament reconstruction surgery in his right (throwing) elbow. Somewhere out there, our two surgeons had to be proud of their work.

The final skill was the handstand walk. Now that was a movement I knew was in my wheelhouse, but I expected Chris Spealler to win the event because of the times I had watched him perform impressively long handstand walks on video. I had a good walk going until I lost my balance and almost fell. I actually could hear the crowd go, "Whoa!" as I regained my balance and continued walking. I won that skill with a walk of 149 feet, 11 inches—more than 25 feet ahead of Chris, who was second. If my feet had touched the ground where I had first lost my balance, I don't know if I would have won or not.

Thanks to some of the other athletes' struggles to land a good softball throw inside the lane, my efforts in the throw and the handstand walk were enough to overcome my L-sit and give me first place in the skills event. Overall, I jumped all the way up to seventh place, with 135 points, only eleven points behind Dan Bailey, who was in first place. (The scoring was changed for 2011, with 100 points being awarded for winning an event, ninety-five for second, ninety for third, and then a sliding scale down through the rest of the finishers. After sixth place, the difference between two places was only two points, and on further down, one point. So an eleven-point deficit was not as large as it would have been in 2010.)

The vast difference in the first two events leveled out the field of competitors in a hurry. Surprisingly nobody finished top ten in both of the events. Dan, for example, had taken the lead by finishing fourth and thirteenth.

So I had survived my poor showing on the beach and my tactical mistake in the L-sit. I was back in the thick of the race before the first day had ended.

And I was so ready for Friday's final event when it was announced. It began with, of all things, a rope climb.

CHAPTER 14

"RICH'S REVENGE"

THE ROPE, THE ROPE, THE ROPE.

For the past year, it had seemed like I couldn't go through a single interview without the rope coming up. I had prevailed against the tree rope outside my cousins' home in Michigan the week after the Games. I also had installed a rope at our CrossFit gym that I worked out on regularly. And a video showing me successfully scaling a rope had made the CrossFit community social media rounds. For eleven-plus months, the rope climb had no longer presented an obstacle for me.

Still, I fielded questions about the rope from media and fans alike in advance of the Games. They all wanted to know whether I was scared that there might be a rope climb in the '11 Games, or if I would be nervous or worried if there was one. I kept saying, "Nope, it's not going to be a problem." I knew, however, that nothing I could say would stop the questions. I would need to *show* that the rope wouldn't be a problem.

Because of the full year's worth of rope-related questions, I was hoping Dave Castro would make the rope climb part of these Games so I could once and for all, on CrossFit's biggest stage, shut down all that talk. I didn't want to just prove I could climb the rope, though; I wanted to win an event that included the rope climb. The fact that the rope climb was part of the very first day made the scenario even better in my eyes.

The day's last event consisted of 5 rounds of fifteen-foot rope climbs followed by reps of clean-and-jerks. On the first round, there would be five ascents on the rope, then one fewer for each following round. The clean-and-jerks would begin with 5 reps at 145 pounds, then drop one rep but add 20 pounds for each ensuing round.

The event began with the rope, and I grabbed hold right away, anchoring my feet in the rope as I had learned through my friend Google and scurrying up to the top like I'd been doing it that way ever since second grade.

I even did one *extra* rope climb, although not by choice. On what I thought would be my last climb, I gave the rig at the top an extra slam with my palm to accentuate finishing the climb. But when I came back to the floor, the judge waved the no-rep signal. We were required to maintain control of the rope during our descent beyond a certain point on the rope, marked with a piece of tape, but I was so pumped I released the rope before reaching the tape.

I was confused at first. I had already started walking toward the barbell for the final rep of clean-and-jerks, but the judge, Bobbi Millsaps, did a good job of stepping in and making it clear right away that I had no-repped—performed the movement improperly. I think I might have briefly voiced my displeasure with Bobbi's ruling, but she made the correct call. I watched a replay later, and I clearly did not maintain control far enough down the rope.

Bobbi is a good judge. The judges are all former competitors or Level 1 seminar staff employees, meaning they know the CrossFit moves well and can recognize what is right and what is not. One thing that's for sure is that if you do disagree with a judge's ruling, you don't have much time to state your case because the clock's still moving and the other competitors are too. The Games aren't like baseball, where all the action stops while a player or manager argues with an umpire.

During the heat of the moment on the stadium floor, my competitive side comes through. If I do think I need to say something to a judge, I'll do so while I am making up the missed rep. But again, Bobbi made the exact call she should have made and handled it well.

The no-rep meant I had to complete an unscheduled sixteenth rope climb, and still I was able to do the one clean-and-jerk rep of 225 pounds and finish first in my heat and, I soon learned, overall for the event. I had won—but by only three seconds over Ben Smith. It was that close, so I benefited from Bobbi being such a good judge and making her decisive call on the rope climb.

Knowing I had done that additional ascent and still finished first made winning the event extra sweet. I was so jacked. The tennis stadium was packed, the crowd was super loud—probably three times louder than the year before—and being under the lights at night had made for an electric atmosphere for an event that some started calling "Rich's Revenge."

"Hey, you *can* climb a rope," Dave teased me as I walked off the floor.

Back in the athletes' area, I was still breathing hard when the first media member asked about the rope climb. It sure was nice to finally hear a positive question about a rope.

Through three events, I was in second place, five points behind Ben. I was asked in an interview while walking to the locker room to give one word to describe how I felt at the end of the first day.

"Blessed," I said. Then, for emphasis, I said it again. "Blessed."

"Why Am I Doing This?"

I left the Home Depot Center that night on an emotional high. I had (I hoped) put the rope-climbing issues to rest once and for all, and after a rough start to the day, I had rallied to move into second place. I felt great but exhausted. I just wanted to go to bed and sleep.

Unfortunately sleep was difficult to come by. I had trouble sleeping throughout the entire weekend. I would lie in bed and think I was about to fall asleep, yet half an hour later I'd still be awake. I had slept great in 2010, but in my second Games, I got about three hours of sleep each night. Sleep is vital to a body's recovery during the Games, and I was coming up short in that category. That was a concern.

Saturday, the second day of competition, is called Moving Day because that's the day when the athletes try to move themselves into a position from which they can make a charge for the championship on Sunday. Because I had moved so much on Friday, climbing into second after placing twenty-sixth in the first event, Saturday was more like Staying Day for me. My goal was to stay at the top of the standings and make sure all the moving took place below me.

When I'm in the position that I was in on Saturday, I can afford to strategize a little. Because the top competitors are placed together in the final heats of each event, and because the competitors in heats are lined up in lanes according to their places in the standings, I simplify the competition to a game of beating the guys next to me. If I can beat the guys in the lanes closest to me, I can either make up points if I'm behind or increase my lead if I'm ahead. The deeper into the competition we get, the less likely it is that someone further down the line will have enough events remaining to make a big run.

Saturday's first event was a four-round triplet with sprints for time: 5 muscle-ups, 10 reps of 245-pound deadlifts, 15 GHD sit-ups, and a sprint that started at fifty yards for the first round and increased by fifty yards each round. I finished second in that event after Josh Bridges, but because Ben Smith placed twelfth, I passed him for the overall lead.

Just keep beating the people next to you, I told myself.

The next event was another three-part skills challenge: two minutes for a one-rep max of a weighted chest-to-bar pull-up, followed by two minutes for a one-rep max of snatch, and then—in one of those "unknown and unknowable" CrossFit Games specials—a sixty-second carry for distance of two weighted five-gallon jugs. I knew Ben was good on snatch, so I wanted to beat him on the pull-up, and I did. I placed fourth and he was seventh. On snatch, I was able to tie Ben for third at 255 pounds. I consider matching him at that skill—one he's very good at—a key moment in the Games for me. I struggled in the jugs carry and finished sixteenth but still ahead of Ben.

Despite my problems with the jugs, I finished tied for second in that overall skills session. Ben was tenth, and with that I opened up my lead over him to fifty-five points, 425 to 370.

Between events, if I have just completed a particularly taxing workout, I like to take an ice bath or spend a few minutes on a rowing machine. In 2011 I added something new for my time between events: reading the Bible app on my phone. Because it gets muggy down on the service level of the stadium, I went back to the top of the stadium, where I had spent time relaxing the year before. Up there, I could sit in the shade and enjoy a nice breeze. Every once in a while, a fan would recognize me and ask to take a photo with me, but for the most part I could just hang out without being interrupted. Depending on how much time I had before needing to warm up for the next event, I would pick up the theme of a recent study or read inspirational verses on my phone.

In addition, I wore inspirational verses on my shoes during the Games. I wrote *Galatians 2:20* on one shoe and *Matthew 27:27-56* on the other. Galatians 2:20 was the verse my friend Donovan had shared with me as being inspiring to him, and the Matthew passage tells the story of Jesus' crucifixion.

When I was tired, beat up, feeling sorry for myself, and asking the *Why am I doing this?* question that frequently pops up during an event, I would answer my own question: *To glorify God.*

The Matthew and Galatians passages served as reminders of what Christ had endured on the cross. He suffered for us, and He died for us to bring us salvation. All I was doing was working out—just participating in a sport. Thinking of what Christ endured on the cross made what I was going through at the time seem like nothing in comparison. Seeing the verses on my shoes kept what I was doing in perspective. *Suck it up,* I'd tell myself. *Keep going.* Christ had done that, and for the greatest cause that ever motivated any man in the history of our world. *Keep going* was the best way I knew to glorify God during my pain in the heat of competition.

The writing on my shoes also raised people's curiosity, producing the same effect as my new tattoo. My shoes provided one more avenue to share my faith with the CrossFit community.

/// CROSSFIT DEFINED ///

GHD SIT-UP

GHD stands for glute-ham developer, a piece of equipment that allows an athlete to work the ab muscles or lower back and upper legs in a highly targeted way. A GHD sit-up involves sitting atop the GHD, lowering your upper body with arms extended over your head till you can touch the floor, then sitting all the way back up.

///

On the Verge—Again

Event 6 was another one of those workouts where I simply did what I needed to do to maintain my position at the top of the leaderboard. The Killer Kage was 3 rounds for time of 7 reps of 225-pound front squats, 700 meters on a Wattbike, and a 100-foot monkey bar traverse. That truly was a killer, coming at the end of the day, especially because the day had started with an emphasis on longevity in the morning triplet combined with the sprint. The front squats were tough, but I banged them out without any problems—my focus on squats during training had paid off. I went as fast as possible on the bike segment, then attacked the monkey bars with increasingly sore hands, finishing sixth. Ben placed nineteenth, giving me a 500 to 419 lead. I took note of Josh Bridges creeping up the leaderboard and into third place close behind Ben, but once again, I had beaten the guy next to me.

The second day ended with me holding an eighty-one-point lead. I overheard it said that I had a "comfortable" lead. I promise you that wasn't said by the person holding that lead. I can't imagine ever feeling comfortable during a CrossFit Games. I mean, I couldn't even get comfortable in my bed that night. Again, I only got three hours of sleep heading into the final events on Sunday. I slept so poorly that I asked Darren, officially designated as my coach so he could have access behind the scenes to be my helper, to attend the early morning athletes' briefing and fill me in later so I could rest a little longer.

On Sunday morning the field was cut to the top twenty-four for the seventh event, a couplet called Dog Sled. The first part of the couplet was 3 rounds of 30 double-unders and 10 reps of 135-pound overhead squats. To complete the couplet, we would do 10 handstand push-ups, push a 465-pound sled forty feet, sprint back to the end of the stadium floor for 10 more HSPUs, return to push the sled forty more feet, go back for the final 10 HSPUs, and then push the sled the remaining forty feet or so to the far end of the stadium.

I was the first one through the double-unders and overhead squats, and I made it through the first handstand push-ups and to the sled a little ahead of Josh Bridges, who started the day in third place. But I slowed on my second round of HSPUs. I couldn't catch up with Josh, and he won the heat and the event. Josh really smoked the Dog Sled, finishing in

4:58. He was impressive. And to show you what a good guy he is, even though he was chasing me in the overall standings, when I was making my final push on the sled, he walked out next to me and urged me on all the way until I touched the end wall with the sled. Then he applauded me and gave me a sweaty man hug.

Josh is an active member of the United States Navy, and it makes me proud knowing that a mentally and physically tough yet kindhearted guy like Josh Bridges is serving our country to help keep us free and protected.

He also is an example of how the presence of community in CrossFit carries over into the competition of the Games. The athletes are friends as well as competitors. CrossFit is the only sport I've been involved in where competitors help each other. If one competitor is struggling with a movement, another will go over to him in the warm-up area and say, "Try this," or "Do it this way." I can't imagine going back to my baseball days and pointing out to a player from the opposing team where he has a hole in his swing.

In the CrossFit Games, the majority of the competitors coach in CrossFit affiliates, so it's natural for us to help others. Though we're competing against each other, sometimes I think we're actually coaches first, and that's cool.

Josh won the event and leapfrogged Ben Smith for second place, but because I came in second, he gained only five points on me, so my lead was eighty-three points going into what we were told a short time later would be, like the conclusion in 2010, a triplet with each segment scored separately.

"The End" would begin with a three-minute AMRAP (which in this case was "as many *reps* as possible"). We had to get as far as we could through a grueling sequence of a 20-calorie row (each calorie burned counted as one rep), 30 wall-ball shots with a 20-pound ball, 20 toes-to-bar, 30 box-jumps with a twenty-four-inch box, 20 sumo deadlift high-pulls with a 108-pound kettlebell, 30 burpees, 20 shoulder-to-overheads with 135 pounds, and a sled pull.

Yes, that was just the first part of The End. After a one-minute rest, the second segment would be a six-minute AMRAP of the same movements. Following a two-minute rest, we would do the same movements again, but for time.

Then, if we survived, the Games would be over.

/// CROSSFIT DEFINED //

SUMO DEADLIFT HIGH-PULL

With your feet apart and your back straight, squat down (like a sumo wrestler) and grasp a weight on the floor (could be a barbell or a kettlebell) with your hands between your feet. Then stand up, thrust your hips forward, and bring the weight all the way up to just below your chin.

///

Adding It All Up

Jeff Barnett, a fellow competitor at the 2010 Regionals whom I had become friends with, called my cell phone before the final event.

"I've done the math," he said. "I know what you have to do to win. Do you want to know?"

"Sure," I said. Jeff told me that I could finish last in the first two AMRAPs and still win the championship by winning the final workout for time.

"What if I beat the guys right behind me?" I asked.

"If you can beat both Ben and Josh in any of the events," Jeff said, "you've won it."

That was all I needed to hear. I immediately set my strategy: win the first AMRAP. I wasn't going to save anything for the end because that's not the CrossFit way. And it's not the Froning way, either.

The field was cut to the top twelve; the final three events would take place in two heats, but the only competitors I needed to keep an eye on were the two guys nearest me in my heat: Ben and Josh. *Beat the guys right next to you.*

When Dave Castro said, "Three, two, one, *go!*" I grabbed the handle on my rower and cranked out a quick 20 calories, then ran over and picked up the wall-ball. I was moving fast but kept my throws under control, hitting the target every time. From there I moved on to the toes-to-bar. When I finished, I looked to the right from my outside lane as I walked to the box-jumps. Blair Morrison, three lanes over, was even with me, but Ben and Josh were still at the toes-to-bar.

No one had made it all the way through the box-jumps when the three-minute time cap expired. During the one-minute break, as we walked back to the starting point for the second leg of the triplet, the public-address announcer called out the number of reps each competitor had completed. Blair had totaled 96 to win the heat, and I was next with 94. I didn't know where that ranked compared to the guys in the first heat, but despite not winning my heat, I had finished ahead of both Josh and Ben. According to what Jeff the mathematician had told me, that should be enough to clinch first place.

I looked across the stadium to where my family and friends were sitting.

Donovan was motioning to me that I had locked up the championship, but Darren was indicating the opposite.

I was confused. I kept looking at them, shrugging to ask where I stood.

You're okay, Donovan kept signaling.

You need to keep going, Darren kept gesturing, right next to Donovan.

I didn't know if I had clinched it or not. I also didn't know that Darren was just messing with me. Darren doesn't care whether we're playing around in our gym or whether it's a crucial moment on the final day of the CrossFit Games—if he sees a chance to get into my head, he's going to try to do it.

Forget it! I told myself. *Either way, you've got to go as hard as you can on this one.*

I won my heat's second AMRAP, getting 23 reps into the burpees before time was called. Without looking into the stands, I was pretty sure I had wrapped up the championship, but I still wasn't 100 percent sure.

Even if I had been positive, there was no way I was going

to turn the final part of the triplet into a victory lap. I was miserable after the first two workouts, but in the back of my mind I considered the possibility that Dave might create some kind of rule at the end that anyone who didn't finish the final event would be disqualified or docked a lot of points or something crazy like that.

So I gave the final workout everything I had, which, truthfully, wasn't a whole lot. I had expended so much energy in the first two AMRAPs that I suffered a bit of a physical and mental crash.

Because the first two workouts had been only three and six minutes long, no one had made it to the sled pull. Oh, my goodness. Talk about a vicious way to end the Games.

The sled was back where we had started the workout, at one end of the stadium. Attached was a rope that covered the length of the floor, and we had to stand at the opposite end and pull the sleds toward us the entire way across the stadium. Josh and Ben, to my left, were just about finished with the sled pull when I started tugging on my rope. I could see Spencer Hendel, across the floor, also was ahead of me.

Keep in mind that the event was taking place on a tennis court. A regulation court is seventy-eight feet long, plus there is all that extra room between the baselines and the seats. The sled weighed 465 pounds. And trust me, it did *not* have wheels on the bottom.

There is a small amount of strategy to the sled pull, but not much. For the most part, it's just a test of strength at the end of three full days of having your strength drained from you.

So there I was at the end of the stadium, pulling the rope to move that stubborn sled across the floor. My family and friends were seated low in that end of the stadium. Apparently they thought the sled should be moving a little faster than I was moving it, because I began to hear from their section, "Pull the sled, Rich! Pull the sled!"

So I pulled. And I pulled. And then I heard again, "Pull the sled! Pull the sled!"

I was thinking sarcastically, *Oh, is that what I'm supposed to do—pull it? Good thing you told me that. I forgot! It completely slipped my mind to pull the sled!*

Finally I'd had enough of their "encouragement," and I stopped pulling, looked at them, and shouted, "I'm trying!"

That is a moment we all laugh about now. But at that time, I couldn't see the humor.

I wouldn't ever want to say my tank is empty during a CrossFit workout, because the mind always has to be able to convince the body to keep going when the body thinks it has nothing left. To me, it's like a car. The fuel gauge can be on E, but the driver knows—or perhaps more appropriately, hopes—that there's always a little extra fuel in the tank. The driver doesn't see the gauge hit E, say, "It's empty," and then pull the car over, turn off the engine, and start pushing. The driver keeps the car going even though the gauge says there's no gas left because the driver *needs* there to be more in the tank to get to a place where he can fuel up again. (I said "he" in this example instead of "he or she" because we all know it's always the man who's running the car below E.) That's how it works with the mind and the body during CrossFit. The body says it's done, but the mind knows there's still a little more in the tank, although, truthfully, the mind can't be certain just how much more there is and how much further the body can go.

When I completed the final workout of the CrossFit Games and knew I was the champion, I would have liked to be able to do some kind of immediate, big celebration. But I was so spent not only from the final workout but also from the entire competition that I couldn't. When I gave the rope the final tug needed to yank the sled across the finish line, Spencer, who had finished his workout and had been beside me encouraging me over my final few pulls, embraced me. I walked the few feet over to the stands and gave the closest thing to a hug I could give my dad as he bent over from the front row. I leaned briefly against the wall, then took a seat on the stadium floor.

Right after you finish a workout in competition, one of the first things you have to do is sign off on your results. Your judge will hand you a sheet of paper with your time or score, and you have to sign to verify that everything is correct. You're doubled over or sitting on the ground or sometimes lying down, trying to catch your breath, soaked with sweat, and then you have to basically sign an autograph. I think half the time I am so physically and emotionally drained that the judge could slip me a note signing over his car loan to me and I'd probably unknowingly sign it. Actually, at that point, I probably wouldn't even care if I did know it was his car loan.

So I sat there, and Ben came over to fist-bump me. Ben had won our heat's final workout going away and wound up finishing third overall behind Josh. Then I heard the PA announcer encouraging the crowd to get behind Dan Bailey. I looked to see that Dan, almost all the way over in the far lane, was the last one in our heat still pulling on a sled. I got to Dan just as he was getting ready to make the final pull to cover the final few feet. With the crowd chanting, "Bailey! Bailey! Bailey!" he leaned back so hard that his butt was on the ground when the sled crossed the line. Dan didn't try to get up. He just lay back on the ground. I leaned over him, gave him a pat on the face, and he briefly and weakly put his arms around me. Believe me, I could feel his pain.

At long last, the competition had concluded. And although the official announcement hadn't been made, I knew I had won.

So how does it feel to be a CrossFit Games champion? To be the Fittest Man on Earth? To have a $250,000 check to deposit?

Mostly I just felt relieved. As disappointing as that answer may sound, relief was my predominant feeling. I was just happy the Games were over. All the physical and mental stress that had been a part of the buildup to the Games was finally behind me.

But I also felt a strong sense of accomplishment. The accomplishment wasn't necessarily winning, although that certainly did add to my feeling because I was in it to win it from the beginning. But my sense of accomplishment, like for the CrossFitters who complete a workout in our gym back home in Cookeville, came from knowing that someone had given me a challenging workout to complete, and I had finished it.

After the medal ceremony, I met up with my family and friends.

"I'm hungry," Hillary said. "Let's go."

That's the exact same thing she had said when she first saw me after the disappointing finish in 2010.

Hillary has a great sense of humor. More important, she doesn't take my CrossFitting too seriously. That was her way of telling me that while she enjoyed watching me win, in the big picture, it didn't matter to her whether I had finished first or second. She's never been one of those caught up with Rich Froning the CrossFitter, and that's exactly what I need.

CHAPTER 15

THE QUEST TO REPEAT

WHAT DO YOU DO after you've won your first CrossFit Games championship? If you're the son of Rich and Janice Froning, you get right back to work preparing for the next Games. And if you've put off your "real" honeymoon, you and your wife go spend a week on a beach.

The big question was whether Games preparation and a honeymoon could coexist.

After a competition, I need more of a mental break than a physical one. Physically I have to keep moving. I'm the type who can't sit still long before I have to get up and move around. I'm constantly flipping something in my hands or playing with something with my fingers. Hillary gets frustrated with me because there's a limited amount of time that I can sit beside her and watch TV before I wind up standing behind the couch or leaning over the back of a chair to watch. That drive to stay active extends to working out. When I don't work out, my body feels worthless.

My solution has been to continue working out after competitions. I'll usually take one complete day off following a Games, but that's about it. What I will do, though, is scale back drastically on the volume of workouts I had been doing leading up to the Games. I might work out twice per day, or maybe just once per day coming out of a Games. But to give myself the needed mental break, I don't put pressure on myself to reach certain times or numbers. Right after going through the pressure cooker of the Games, workouts have to be fun, or I won't want to do them.

But back to the honeymoon issue. I didn't think I could just completely shut down the workouts, so, I confess, I got creative. When Hillary would take a shower, I'd sneak in a quick workout that was just enough to feel active. I had a kettlebell in our hotel room, and while Hillary was showering, I'd do some kettlebell swings and kettlebell front squats in our room or out on the deck. As far as I know, Hillary wasn't aware I was sneaking in workouts on our honeymoon. There is a good chance that she didn't find out until she read this page.

One great thing about being a newlywed after winning the Games was the travel opportunities that came through my Reebok sponsorship. Before the 2010 Games, I had never been west of Texas. The extent of my travels was trips home to Michigan, spring breaks in Florida, and a job interview for my dad in Texas. In the fall after winning the Games, my new bride and I were able to visit Europe, South Korea, and Mexico to promote Reebok and CrossFit.

I had met international competitors at the Games, but it was amazing to see the large numbers of people in the countries we visited who were into CrossFit. I knew CrossFit had gone global, but those tours opened my eyes to just how global. The trips also gave me a preview of some of the competition that could be coming in future Games, because there were people all around the world aiming to win the title I had just claimed. I knew from my own experience how in only a few months someone could progress from unknown CrossFitter to Games championship contender.

Fall is my slow time—relatively speaking—for training, but I work out year-round and usually multiple times per day. As a result, in the aftermath of the Games, I had to make sure I worked training into my travel schedule. One of CrossFit's appeals is that many of its workouts can be done anywhere. If a CrossFitter is traveling and in a place that does not have equipment, there are still enough movements that don't require equipment that he or she can get in full workouts. Of course, part of my duties on the foreign trips was to work out with CrossFitters at their affiliates. It was crazy to think that I basically was traveling *to* work out. To this day, I'm still amazed that I work out for a living.

Since I was the reigning CrossFit champion and came from America, the foreign CrossFitters were curious to watch me work out and talk with me about the sport. I've already mentioned that talking in public does not come naturally to me. I'm not afraid of heights, I've ridden bulls (live bulls, not mechanical ones), I've jumped out of an airplane, and I've run into burning buildings as a firefighter. When I was a kid, I didn't think twice about rappelling down a 20-foot bluff with a water hose. But stand up in front of people and speak? No thanks.

Well, I had to get over that in a hurry.

Another area of discomfort for me is working out in front of people. Training with workout partners is one thing, but I don't like to work out with people just watching. I don't know why, but I don't feel right having spectators hanging around. That includes family, too. But as with public speaking, I had to quickly adapt to being outside of my comfort zone with the public workouts.

The way I learned to look at it, the public workouts and talks weren't about me. The opportunities came to me as ways to promote CrossFit and Reebok, but I realized that because people were curious about me, these were also opportunities to tell who I was—not Rich Froning the CrossFitter but Rich Froning the Christian. The Galatians tattoo on my side helped with that.

I thought of the stories about Tim Tebow, when he would write *John 3:16* on his eye black while playing football at the University of Florida. During his games on television, *John 3:16* would rank as the number one search on Google. I had decided to get my Galatians 6:14 tattoo solely for myself, but as I and the tattoo became more visible through the Games, I started fielding lots of questions about what Galatians 6:14 meant. After all, it's not nearly as well-known of a verse as John 3:16, and I enjoyed being asked so I could tell what the verse meant to me.

Funny story: In one interview during a Games, while I was rowing to cool down from an event, I was asked about my "Galactica" tattoo. I chuckled and told the interviewer that the tattoo said *Galatians*. "It's a Bible verse," I told him. "You should look it up."

It was while we were traveling in Mexico with Reebok that Hillary and I bought our first home back in Cookeville. We were living in a two-bedroom apartment when we found a foreclosed house that we liked. We submitted a bid, but it wasn't accepted and the house went to auction. The auction was scheduled for while we were in Mexico, and we asked my dad to attend and bid for us with strict instructions not to go over $140,000. We had crunched the numbers and determined that was as high as we could go.

In Mexico we had to borrow a cell phone from one of the Reebok reps who had an international plan. Hillary and I were texting back and forth with my dad during the auction, but we lost our connection. When we got a signal again, there was a text waiting from Dad, asking if we were willing to go to $145,000.

We figured we didn't have much time to discuss it, so we quickly shot back to Dad to go for it.

Too late, Dad answered. *Already did it.*

The house was ours.

"Honey, Meet Dan"

Not long after we bought our house, Dan Bailey, one of the guys I had competed against in the Games, came to Cookeville to interview for a graduate assistant position with Chip Pugh at Tennessee Tech.

Dan worked at Rogue Fitness in Columbus, Ohio, and Thomas Cox and I had first met him at the 2011 Regionals when I was competing with Thomas on the CrossFit Faith team. I had talked to Dan a little bit at the Games, but he and Thomas had become friends because they both had been part of Athletes in Action and had other activities in common.

Thomas, an assistant coach at Tennessee Tech, led devotions for the football team, and after Regionals, he had asked Dan if he would come to Cookeville and lead a devotion.

While Dan was on campus, he, Chip, and I were talking, and Dan told Chip that he would be interested in taking a GA position if one opened because he wanted to finish up his master's degree.

Pretty soon after Dan returned home to Columbus, a GA position opened up. Dan came back to Cookeville to interview with Chip, and he got the job. After the successful interview, Dan stopped by our house, and I asked where he was going to live. Dan said he hadn't had a chance yet to look for an apartment but that Thomas had offered to let him stay with his family until he found his own place.

I informed Dan that Thomas and his wife had a three-year-old and a newborn. "I don't know if you want to do that," I advised him.

Then I told Dan that we had two rooms upstairs and he could stay with us until he found a place to live. The next weekend, Dan moved in with a blow-up mattress, a lawn chair, and a computer.

That was in November 2011. As of this writing, Dan is still staying with us temporarily until he finds his own place!

I get asked about Dan often. Apparently people think it's unusual for two Games competitors to be living under the same roof. CrossFit also filmed a nice video about Dan, me, and our faith that resulted in positive feedback for both of us.

In addition to Dan being a world-class athlete I could train with, having him move in immediately paid other dividends. Dan's a good dude, but truth be told, he is a mess. He leaves lights on, and he leaves his clothes and whatever else all around the house. I have to follow along behind Dan and pick up after him. Having Dan around is like having a kid in the house. In fact, Dan is preparing Hillary and me well for when we have our own children. Anyway, Dan's messiness means that I have a perfect scapegoat whenever I need one. If I do something around the house that I know Hillary won't like, I can say, "Dan did it" and avoid trouble. Or at least not get into as much trouble as I should. Of course, Hillary doesn't fall for it anymore, so the tactic is less effective than it used to be.

Hillary didn't actually meet Dan until the day he moved

in with us. I told her how Dan had no place to stay and that all he had was a mattress, lawn chair, and computer.

"Of course he should stay here," Hillary said.

Hillary and Dan hit it off right away, and since the start, they have gotten along so much like a brother and a sister that their play fights are free entertainment for me. That's not the number one reason I enjoy having Dan living with us, but it does help.

If It Ain't Broke . . .

I didn't change my strategy for preparing for the 2012 Games. It had worked in 2011, so why mess with it? I placed an emphasis on continuing to get stronger through Olympic lifting, but other than that, I basically stayed with the same routine—or lack thereof—as the year before.

I had the same level of motivation, too. Winning in 2011 did nothing to reduce my desire to win in 2012. One interviewer in particular seemed to have a difficult time believing that I could be equally hungry to win in 2012 as I had been the year before. I was working out during the interview, and I was baffled by his line of questioning. But I think I can now explain having the same desire to win by saying that winning wasn't my ultimate goal in 2011, and it wasn't my ultimate goal the next year, either. My number one goal was to glorify God through my competing. I could do that whether I was a champion, came in second again, or finished out of the top ten. I suppose the interviewer and I had different perspectives on what the Games meant to me.

But that being said, I still wanted to win just as much as before.

Dave Castro had said that there would never be a repeat champion at the Games. I grew up a Detroit Lions fan and witnessed Hall of Famer Barry Sanders play running back about as well as anyone in the history of the National Football League. One of the numerous impressive things about Barry was that as great of a player as he was, he never acted like he could claim any greater status than any other player on the roster. Barry preferred to talk about his team more than himself. He didn't overcelebrate when he gained a first down, and when he scored a touchdown, he simply handed the ball to an official instead of spiking it and doing some kind of crazy watch-me end-zone dance. It was said of Barry when he was in the end zone that he acted like he'd been there before. I liked that and wanted to emulate his quiet confidence.

I'm not a trash-talker (except with my cousins, but that's family and doesn't count). I already don't want to be the person wearing the target for others to take aim at, and I don't try to bring attention to myself with bold claims. So I didn't say anything to Dave about his prediction that no one would ever go back-to-back at the Games. I didn't say a lot about it to anyone in the media either. But Dave's comment did motivate me.

CrossFit changed its rules in 2012 and required everyone to go through all the qualifying rounds, removing the free pass to the Games I had received in 2011. That meant that just like every other CrossFit competitor around the world, I had to go through the five-week Open from late February through March to qualify for the Central East Regional in May. Notably, the total number of participants in 2012 was more than double the number from the previous year!

For each workout, CrossFit HQ went on location with one or two Games athletes and filmed them doing that week's workout to demonstrate the proper standards that judges would be looking for. Dan and I were featured for the second week's workout. The video was shot in the weight room at Tennessee Tech. With Dave Castro wearing a CrossFit Faith T-shirt, we went through a ten-minute AMRAP—all five Open workouts were AMRAPs—consisting of 30 snatches at 75 pounds, 30 snatches at 135 pounds, 30 snatches at 165 pounds, and as many snatches as we could work in at 210 pounds. They had Dan and me facing each other about seven or eight feet apart during the workout. We matched each other rep for rep until about the final minute. I ended up with 98 reps, barely more than Dan. That score ended up being the top number in that workout out of all the Open participants around the world.

I finished in the top three in four of the five workouts— all except the first one, which was seven minutes of burpees. I placed thirty-fourth in that one with 141 reps, and I actually think it's pretty cool that thirty-three people around the world are able to brag that they beat the CrossFit Games champion in that event. When the dust settled at the end of it all, I had finished the Open in first place, comfortably earning another trip to Regionals.

A "Games" before the Games

Between the Open and Regionals, BSN Supplements offered me an endorsement contract, and that created a potential conflict at Tennessee Tech. The NCAA rightly must be careful about athletes using drugs and supplements of any kind, whether legal or illegal, healthy or unhealthy. There were no issues with the supplements I used and would be endorsing, but still, since I was a coach, I realized it would be a sensitive area. I faced a choice: leave Tech or turn down the endorsement deal. BSN was offering about twice my salary at the university, so I resigned my job. The income from the BSN deal also lightened my schedule to where I wouldn't have to fit in my workouts around coaching.

The Central East turned out to be a stacked region. The competition took place in Columbus, Ohio. Graham Holmberg, the 2010 champion, lives in Ohio, and I live in Tennessee, so the past two Games champions would be competing in the same region. Add in Dan Bailey, and amazingly, with seventeen regions around the world, including ten in the United States, three of the top six finishers at the 2011 Games were in one region.

Dan set the tone for what would be an intense three days of competition when he demolished the world record with a time of 1:35 in Diane, which consists of 21-15-9 reps of

225-pound deadlifts and handstand push-ups. I finished in 2:14—thirty-nine seconds behind Dan—good enough for fifth place.

Broken world records would prove to be the norm at the Central East Regionals, with new records set in five of the six events. I broke the world record in the next event—a 2,000-meter row, 50 pistols, and 30 hang cleans with 225 pounds—to tighten up the points race. The first day ended with Dan in first with five points and Graham and me tied one point behind him.

Just as he had on Friday, Dan started Saturday with a world-record performance when he won the dumbbell snatch event—4 rounds for time of 10 one-arm dumbbell snatches of 100 pounds followed by a short sprint across the arena floor—in a time of 3:22. Graham placed second, and I placed third to leave myself three points behind Dan.

Halfway through the six events, the three of us were beginning to put some separation between us and the rest of the field, setting up a three-man race for the top prize. It was time for me to kick it into gear, and I did. I won the final three events, setting world records in two of them.

It started with the fourth event, which was a crazy combination of squats, pull-ups, and shoulder-to-overheads: 50 back squats of 135 pounds, 40 pull-ups, 30 shoulder-to-overheads of 135 pounds, 50 front squats of 85 pounds, 40 pull-ups, 30 shoulder-to-overheads of 85 pounds, 50 overhead squats of 65 pounds, 40 pull-ups, and 30 shoulder-to-overheads of 65 pounds. My time in that event was 15:29, and that allowed me to take the overall lead at the end of the second day with ten points—three ahead of Dan and six ahead of Graham.

I really liked Sunday's two events, especially the first one, which was a snatch ladder with double-unders. We had fifty seconds to complete 20 double-unders and a snatch on each step of the ladder of ascending-weight barbells. The ladder started at 155 pounds and increased in 10-pound increments up to the 295-pound max. I topped out at 275 pounds, and I was the only competitor to reach that weight. Dan finished third, and that sent us into the final event with me leading him by five points and Graham by thirteen.

The final event consisted of 3 rounds of 7 deadlifts (345 pounds) and 7 muscle-ups, followed by 3 rounds of 21 wall-balls and 21 toes-to-bar, and concluding with a farmer's carry of two 100-pound dumbbells, 28 burpee box-jumps, another farmer's carry, and 3 muscle-ups. As the overall leader, I was in lane one, and Dan was immediately to my left in lane two.

Dan took a slight early lead that he was able to hold on me until the end of the first round of wall-balls. We moved to the toes-to-bar at almost exactly the same time, and by the end of the 21 reps, I had passed him up. The farmer's carry, where we carried the barbells across the arena floor, was the first real opportunity to measure what kind of lead I had, and I felt fairly comfortable with my lead when I reached the burpee box-jump and could see Dan back getting ready to start his farmer's carry.

But Dan being Dan, he started cutting into my lead during the jumps. That's the way we are—close friends, but we push each other. We don't make things easy for the other guy. The announcer was calling our reps on the jumps, and Dan got to within 3 or 4 reps of me at one point. But I think the pace he had to do to try to catch up started to take its toll on him a little more than halfway through.

When I finished my jumps and picked up the barbells for the final carry to the muscle-ups, I had my sights set on the world record of 13:24 held by Ben Smith. The announcer was doing everything he could to keep the crowd pumped up, and as he was calling out the time, I knew I had the record beaten. I finished off the workout at the 12:22 mark and was able to cheer on Dan when he started his 3 muscle-ups. Dan had a chance at finishing ahead of Ben's record too, so I was really encouraging him. And he did it, with a time of 13:06.

Because of the high-caliber athletes in the Central East, winning the Regional felt like I had won a Games from a competitive standpoint. Dan finished second, and Graham was third. According to CrossFit rules, only the top three finishers from each Regionals competition advance to the Games, but if a former champion takes one of the qualifying spots, the next-best finisher from that region also goes through. In 2012, with *two* past champions claiming two of the qualifying spots, Marcus Hendren and Scott Panchik—the fourth- and fifth-place finishers—also were awarded Games invitations. All five of us wound up in the top ten at the Games. That's just crazy—and that's why I say it felt like I had won a Games instead of a Regional.

/// CROSSFIT DEFINED /////////////////////////////////////

FARMER'S CARRY
The farmer's carry is an example of the kind of practical movement that can be included in a CrossFit workout. In this exercise, you carry something heavy in each hand while walking some distance, just like a farmer carrying bales of hay or jugs of water from the barn to the field.

HANG CLEAN
For a hang clean, you begin the clean movement holding the bar at waist level. This is different from a power clean, where the weights have to touch the ground between each rep.

///

CHAPTER 16

THE LONGEST DAY

WE SHOULD HAVE KNOWN something was up when CrossFit HQ released the Games schedule along with descriptions of more than half of the individual events on the Friday before the week of the Games. In 2010 we had been told what the events would be right before we had to do each one. In 2011 we were told about an hour ahead of time. Yet now the events were being announced a full week in advance. Details were given to us about two of the three events on Friday and three of the four events on Saturday. Sunday's events were listed only as *TBA*.

There was one major surprise, though, during Monday's pre-Games dinner for all the competitors.

As Dave Castro wrapped up his customary address to the competitors, during which he goes over whatever details need to be covered before the Games and gets a jump start on getting inside our heads a little, he said he had "one more thing."

Dave began by talking about Reebok's sponsorship and that he had taken note of how Reebok had been good about giving the athletes shoes and great gear. Then he said he had begun questioning why CrossFit wasn't giving anything to its athletes. That was about to change, he said. CrossFit had a couple of gifts it wanted to present to each of us: a pair of swim fins and a mountain bike.

That set up Dave announcing that an event was being added to the schedule: the first ever CrossFit Games triathlon. The event would consist of a 700-meter swim with fins, an eight-kilometer bike ride, and an eleven-kilometer run up and down a mountain.

The immediate reaction throughout the room was laughter, but it wasn't a *That Dave sure is funny* kind of laughter. It was a nervous laughter. There were some eyes opening wide and some jaws dropping, for sure.

I think my reaction was simply *Huh?* In my short time of Games competitions, I had come to expect the unexpected, but the triathlon announcement was my first true you've-got-to-be-kidding-me surprise at a Games.

There was more. Not only was a triathlon being added, but the triathlon also would be scored as two events. The swim-bike portion would count as the first event, and the run would be the second event. But there would be no break in between. The swim-bike and the run would be continuous but separate events, and the clock would not be reset between events. In other words, we would receive points based on where we were at the end of the swim-bike and then again after the run. A poor start in the swim-bike could be doubly harmful to an athlete's point total.

In the three-day schedule that had been released earlier, there was no room for a CrossFit triathlon away from the Home Depot Center. Dave was asked the obvious question: When?

"Your CrossFit Games," Dave answered, "start Wednesday." Then he informed us that the triathlon would take place at Camp Pendleton, the US Marine Corps's largest West Coast base.

I didn't know much about Camp Pendleton, but I had heard enough to know that this wasn't going to be a leisurely swim, bike, and run alongside families at a nearby recreational lake.

So the Games were going to start two days earlier than expected with an off day on Thursday before what we had been told was coming Friday through Sunday.

The change in schedule didn't bother me, but I would have preferred the selection of a different first event—officially, the first two events. A triathlon was about as far out of my comfort zone as the Games could possibly get. My triathlon experience consisted entirely of one that our training group, including Dan, had created for ourselves at a lake not far from Cookeville. That was a 600-meter swim, a 38-mile bike, and a five-kilometer run, and we had geared it more toward being fun than a competition.

On Tuesday we were taken to a local beach for a test swim with our fins and also allowed to try out our bikes. It was funny at the beach because Jason Khalipa started in with his typical joking around. Jason's a big ol' goofball— that's typically a compliment, by the way, when someone from Tennessee says it—and he started talking like he was an expert about the size of the swells while we were there and how they were expected to be twice as large where we would be competing the next day.

I looked at Jason like *Come on, man. I'm not that stupid. I know what you're doing.*

But there were some guys who didn't know Jason well and I assumed had to be from someplace like Nebraska or Oklahoma, because their big-eyed looks were shouting, *I'm going to die in the Pacific Ocean!*

I had a full day to look ahead to the triathlon, and that was a day when having placed twenty-sixth in the first event of 2011 helped me. I had overcome that slow start, and I knew that if I met my low expectations for the triathlon and got off to another bad start, I could still come back to win. There still was an entire load of events Friday through Sunday during which I could make up whatever ground I needed to.

In a nutshell, I told myself, there was nothing I could do about the triathlon events being part of the Games. I couldn't change the schedule, but I had worked diligently to prepare for the Games. Despite my concern about the triathlon, I felt an all-encompassing calmness that was even greater than the feeling I had at the start of the 2011 Games after reading Jeremiah 29:11-13.

But still, I wondered what would happen out there.

The men's and women's competitors boarded two buses at 5 a.m. on a foggy and cool Wednesday morning to head to the first event. It was mostly quiet on my bus during the 80-mile ride. Some were sleeping, and some were quietly taking in the scenery along the route, although I assumed most in that latter group were actually getting into competition mode instead of enjoying the scenery. There's a buildup among the competitors that can be sensed at the beginning of a Games, and starting on a bus ride brought all the individuals' energy together into one place. It was a much more intense feeling than starting the Games inside a stadium locker room.

Camp Pendleton

All right, let's do this, I thought as I stepped off the bus.

Of course, Dave being Dave, we couldn't just start the swim-bike-run by swimming. We first had to run 400 meters across the beach, swim fins in hand, to get to the swim start point. Yep, another lovely soft-sand run. Fortunately the fog had lifted and the sun had come up before we hit the ocean, so the temperature wasn't as cool as when we arrived.

I swam well and came out of the water alongside Dan,

which seemed fitting considering how many times we had swum together in a pond at my dad's place during the wintertime so we could get our bodies and minds accustomed to cold swims. After grabbing our bikes and setting off on the eight-kilometer ride, we quickly discovered that the bike ride would not be all riding. After a half-mile flat ride on pavement, we transitioned to a trail and immediately had to push our single-speed bikes more than half a mile through sand too soft to ride on. Even when we could ride our bikes, the mixed terrain was rough until we hit a flat, paved route about three and a half miles long for a sprint to the end of the first event.

The run portion took us up and away from the ocean, climbing more than 1,400 feet in a little more than two miles to near the mountain's summit. We ran mostly on dirt roads with loose rocks and gravel, forcing us to be cautious with our footing. One problem we had came from not knowing the lay of the land. We would go up a hill, only to reach the top and find a climb to another hill ahead of us. We couldn't get perspective on how near we were to the summit and the start of our descent.

I was running in a group that included Dan, Jason Khalipa, Austin Malleolo, Christy Phillips, and Annie Sakamoto (the men's and women's triathlons were held simultaneously), and we brainstormed and decided that roughly every minute we would run for twenty seconds and then walk the rest of the minute. It was fun following that plan as a group. We were competing against each other, but we were also taking a let's-get-through-this-together mentality.

Austin wanted to run more frequently, and after each run,

he kept saying, "Let's do it again." The rest of us would be like "Ehhhh." Finally Austin and a couple of others decided to break out of the pack and took off running. The rest of us let them go.

I had planned on staying with the pack that remained, but when we reached the top and knew we had finished our climb, instead of running and walking in timed intervals, I wanted to run downhill and walk uphill. I wasn't sure what would happen if I followed that strategy, but there was only one way to find out.

Running downhill was tough because of the terrain. In addition to the steep ascent, the course had a pretty steep drop, too. I saw some guys running portions of the downhill backward to balance out the strain on their leg muscles. Others turned their bodies and feet at an angle to slow their forward momentum.

My decision to break away from the pack turned out to be a good one because I passed probably twelve people on the back side of the run. I passed some who were cramping and some who looked like they were about to drop. I don't know if it was because I had saved enough energy during the climb or what, but I actually felt good on the descent. I didn't have any cramping, and the only problem I had was a small blister developing on one foot.

I gained ground on the run portion. I was eighteenth (fifty-one points) after the swim-bike event, finishing that portion of the race in a time of 48:59, but I was twelfth after the run (sixty-five points for the second event) with a total time of two hours and six minutes. That was enough to place me thirteenth after the first two events—far better than twenty-sixth, that's for sure.

Being in thirteenth was better than I had anticipated. Apparently it was better than expected for my biggest supporters, too. When I got to my phone later, I had a load of text messages from family and friends saying I had done better on the triathlon than they had thought I would. Thanks, guys!

The triathlon was the longest event in CrossFit Games history, and I could tell as the athletes were recovering in ice baths that the triathlon had taken its toll. Chris Spealler was battling awful leg cramps that had slowed him during the run and was getting an IV, and Numi Katrinarson—the coleader after getting first place in the swim-bike and finishing second in the run—had felt like he was about to faint and was taken to a hospital. The emergency room doctor told Numi he should stay overnight for observation, but Numi left the hospital and came back in time to take part in the next event.

The O-Course

It took close to three hours for the triathlon to complete, and Dave graciously gave us a whole hour after the final finisher to rest up for the next event: the Marines' School of Infantry obstacle course.

We ran the same obstacle course as the Marines—minus the muscle pull-ups and one of my new favorites, the rope climb—in a tournament-style, elimination-bracket format.

I won my first-round four-man heat to advance to the semifinals, where I caught a break. Lucas Parker had about a twenty-foot lead over me and Neal Maddox halfway through the course, but Lucas had a hiccup going over the five-foot-high log, and Neal and I caught up to him. Lucas then fell coming out of the next-to-last log jump, and Neal's foot caught on the final log jump and he fell a few steps from the finish line. Their falls enabled me to advance to the finals.

I thought the obstacle course favored taller athletes, which worried me because I'm a hair shy of five foot ten. Plus, the other three competitors in the final heat were Spencer Hendel, Kenneth Leverich, and Pat Burke. Spencer and Kenneth had turned in superfast times in the earlier rounds, and Pat was a former Marine who had once held the Camp Pendleton O-course record. Considering that before the first round I was hoping to make it into the top sixteen, I was already pleased knowing I could do no worse than fourth place. Pat, though, had a slipup in the final race, and I was able to sneak into third place and take the ninety points. I left the O-course feeling like I had swiped a few points.

At the end of the first day, I was in fifth place with 204 points. Chad Mackay was in first with 242 points, so I was in pretty close range to him. Physically I was wiped out. The O-course, which I ran three times, was a short-burst workout, but we all were still feeling the effects of the triathlon when we boarded the bus to leave Camp Pendleton and head back to our hotel and an off day before starting the regular three days of competition at the Home Depot Center.

CHAPTER 17

NO DOUBT

Running the Camp Pendleton obstacle course had been a cool opportunity that most people aren't able to experience. It was an honor to traverse the same O-course used by great men and women who have served our country. That honor was followed by an event on Friday morning that was right out of an elementary school field day competition: the broad jump.

The broad jump originally was scheduled to be held at Camp Pendleton but had been pushed back to Friday. I didn't know why, although I heard both that it was because we were all too fatigued from the triathlon and because we were running out of daylight at Camp Pendleton.

In a change to the sliding points scale for 2012, three events had been designated as fifty-point events, with the top finisher earning fifty points instead of one hundred. The broad jump was the first of those three.

We started underneath the seats, before fans had entered the stadium. The broad jump was a movement that would measure our explosive jumping ability and hip extension. It wasn't going to be one of my better events to begin with, and on my first jump I could still feel some of the hangover from the triathlon in my leg muscles. My best jump of 104 inches tied for sixteenth and earned me thirty-one points. My first priority had been to survive that event points-wise, and I lost only a bit of ground to Kyle Kasperbauer, who finished two spots ahead of me and overtook Chad Mackay for the lead with 274 points.

After lunch, our first event in front of fans—other than the few Marines who had gathered to watch us on their O-course—was the ball toss, and the stands at the track venue were packed. The ball toss was another fifty-point event. We had to sit on a GHD, lean back to pick up a four-pound medicine ball off the ground from a special rack behind us, sit up, and throw the medicine ball as far as we could. Scoring zones were marked on the field, and the point values increased with distance. We would have twenty seconds to throw as many balls as we could to score as many points as we could.

Before the ball toss, a Games official told me I would have to turn my headband inside out.

The headband actually was part of a black T-shirt I had cut off and wore around my forehead to keep sweat from dripping into my eyes. On the front I had written, *Psalm 23*. On the sides I had written the initials of my grandmother, my cousins Donnie and Matt, and Chad Robinson, a high school friend and football teammate. Chad had asked for my help with his fitness and had used our gym's website to guide his workouts. Chad had a young son, and his wife was pregnant again when he was killed in a car accident while on his way home from work.

The memories of those four were important to me when I competed, because when my body would want to stop and I could sense my mind was about to tell my body it was okay to take a break, thoughts of them inspired me to keep going.

I had competed with a Scripture reference and initials on my headband previously, and when I asked why suddenly I was being told to turn it inside out, the answer was that the order had come "down from the top."

CrossFit officials had wanted to take care of Reebok as the Games' title sponsor, and I agreed with that. Any "non-permanent branding" was not allowed so as not to infringe on Reebok's sponsorship rights, and I had seen other athletes having to place tape over various brands on their clothing. In my opinion, however, the initials on my headband did not create any competitive marketing problems for Reebok, with which, after all, I had an endorsement contract.

That afternoon I was able to present my case to a Reebok official, who told me, "You're fine. Flip it right-side out." But that was later. I had to wear my headband inside out for the ball toss and the track triplet that followed. That really ticked me off and supplied me with an extra dose of motivation heading into the ball toss.

The key in that event was to throw as many balls as possible within the twenty seconds, and making that rapid movement repeatedly put enough strain on the abdominal muscles to make anyone who had eaten a full lunch lose it right there on the spot. I could tell I had done well based on where my balls were grouped down the field compared to the other competitors' balls at the end of the heat. In fact, I was surprised I had done as well as I appeared to have done. But there was no time to learn I had finished third in the event, because the twelve guys in our final heat headed directly to the track for the track triplet: 3 rounds for time of 8 split snatches of 115 pounds, 7 bar muscle-ups, and a 400-meter run.

As I came off the final bar muscle-ups for the last 400-meter run, Matt Chan had a slight lead on me. On the backstretch, I could sense that Matt was tiring a little, and I started gaining on him. I passed him on the curve and was clear of him coming out of the final turn. Matt made a run at me down the backstretch, but I was able to hold him off and beat him by one second. One fun thing about the Games is that in that situation, Matt and I weren't racing just each other. We were well ahead of everyone else in our heat, but we also were racing unseen opponents: the guys with the top times in the previous heats. I finished fourth overall with a time of 8:15.6.

But I had slowed in my final steps to the finish line. If I had finished nine-tenths of a second sooner, I would have placed second instead of fourth. Despite those two places I didn't gain, my ball toss and track triplet performances were enough to move me into first place just ahead of Kyle Kasperbauer, 366 to 354, with Matt close behind at 353.

I was surprised to be in first. Most of the events to that point hadn't featured my stronger movements. Looking ahead, I saw that good events for me were coming up. Still, I was frustrated because even though I was sitting in first place, I had yet to win an event.

Friday's final event was the Medball-HSPU. Because I was in first place, I was the last athlete introduced for our heat. Dave Castro came over to me and, never one to miss an opportunity to rib me, asked, "You're already in first? I didn't expect you to be in first yet."

"Yeah, funny," I told him.

Medball-HSPU consisted of 3 rounds, for time, of 8 medicine-ball cleans at 150 pounds, a 100-foot medicine ball carry, 7 parallette handstand push-ups, and another 100-foot ball carry. In other words, we had to hoist a 150-pound ball up over our shoulder, let it drop to the ground, then turn, pick it up, and do it again, eight times. Then we had to lift it up to our shoulder again and run with it across the stadium to where parallettes were set up, do 7 handstand push-ups on the parallettes, pick the heavy ball back up, and bring it back to where we started.

I wasn't sure I'd be able to hold on to first place in the

Medball-HSPU because I anticipated potentially slowing down on the handstand push-ups. My numbers say handstand push-ups historically aren't a bad movement for me, but I knew from my time working out alongside Dan, who is incredible at them, that they aren't something I look forward to with a lot of confidence.

As I was strategizing about the event with Ben Smith beforehand, he recommended not running out of breath on the first round of medball cleans to save ourselves for the first set of handstands. But after my sixth medball clean, that plan was out the window because I was already short on breath. The handstand push-ups didn't go nearly as bad as I thought they might, primarily because I was able to pace myself well enough to minimize the number of no-reps, and I won our heat with a time of 6:59.4. Kyle finished second in our heat, and overall I placed fourth and Kyle fifth. That increased my lead over him by five points more, 451 to 434. Matt finished twenty-fourth in the event and lost significant ground to both of us, with Chad Mackay passing him for third with 403 points.

Putting a little bit of extra distance between Kyle and me was a great way to end the night.

One of the things I love best about the CrossFit community is the way competitors encourage each other. I've benefited from that, and I try to return the favor whenever I can. When I was done with my final medball carry, I jogged back across the stadium and cheered on Graham Holmberg as he muscled through his final set of HSPUs.

/// **CROSSFIT DEFINED** //

SPLIT SNATCH
Perform a snatch, catching the bar overhead in a split position with
one foot forward and one foot back. Then bring your feet together
while holding the bar in a locked-out position.

//

Rough Sledding

Adding to my lead during Friday's last event put me in position to do what I like to do most in competitions: focus on
beating the guy next to me.

Saturday began with a couplet—a sprint (the final fifty-
point event), followed by a one-minute break, and then a
rope climb–sled combination. The sprint was fifty yards
down and back and then one hundred yards down and back.
Dan Bailey, one of the fastest guys I know, crushed the sprint,
but I made a strategy mistake. I was concerned about the
second workout of the couplet, so I conserved energy. Kyle,
running to my right, beat me by a fraction of a second, and
I lost probably a couple of other places in my heat alone
because I chose not to push all the way through to the finish
line. That was another case where one event led directly into
the other and we weren't aware of how we had finished in
the sprint, and that was a good thing because I would have
been upset with myself if I had known I'd placed eighteenth.

I knew the rope climb and sled—5 rounds of a twenty-
foot climb and a twenty-yard sled drive—was going to be a

beating, but not because of the rope. My performance on the rope climb in 2011 had taken care of all the rope questions. Well, not all of them, but the questions were completely different in 2012. I don't anticipate that the rope questions will ever go away entirely. But instead of the questions focusing on whether I would be able to climb the rope or if I had any fears or worries about the event, they tended to acknowledge the success I'd had in overcoming the rope problem the year before. It was good to have that issue resolved, at least as much as it could be resolved.

The problem was the sled. The sleds were the kind that football players use to practice blocking and tackling, and they are heavy! I knew I was in for a fight when I came down from my first rope climb. I lowered my right shoulder and drove into the padding, and the sled lurched forward—but not as easily or as far as I wanted it to. We had practiced with the sleds during Thursday's off day, but somehow between then and Saturday afternoon the sleds must have gotten heavier.

I don't know if there had been a little rain or if the field inside the track had been watered or what. The field was slightly crowned in the middle for draining purposes, and because I was in lane one, I was where the field leveled off below the crown and near the sideline. Whatever the reason, it seemed the ground was extremely soft.

I was able to finish the first twenty yards without having to stop, but I also was fighting the sled the entire way. After another rope climb, I made it through the second twenty-yard push about like I had made it through the first.

But when I came back for the third push on the sled, I could have sworn that while I was on the rope, someone had put extra weight on the sled. It did not want to go anywhere. It wasn't that my legs were that tired—they felt fine. It's just that the sled didn't seem to want to move. Matt Chan was out ahead of me three lanes over, and I stopped and saw how he was lifting up on the sled as he pushed. So I gave that a try, and the sled started moving better, but it still was taking everything I had in me to keep it going forward.

It only got worse from there. The fourth round, the sled felt like someone had put spikes on the bottom so it would dig into the ground when I was pushing. The fifth round felt like trying to push a parked car with the emergency brake engaged. By that point, Matt had finished. He was about the length of the field ahead of me when I came down from the rope the final time, and before I made contact with the sled for the last twenty yards, I pointed over to Matt to indicate to him that I was impressed. When I did finally push my parked car across the finish line, my hamstrings, calves, quads, glutes, and a few other muscle groups were barking at me. It was difficult to breathe, too, because pushing on the sled had pressed my diaphragm against my lungs.

The sled was an all-around miserable experience. My entire rope-sled workout lasted 9:12.2, and when I reached the end, I crumpled to the grass and rolled over onto my back, trying to find air somewhere to breathe in. The only nine minutes of my sports life that had felt longer was in 2010 when I couldn't figure out how to climb the rope.

That had been a time of trying to figure out technique. This had simply been flat-out physical exertion like I had never experienced. I wasn't the only one suffering, though, because I watched as others would finish and collapse next to their sleds at the finish line.

For that event, there weren't guys hopping up and going across the field to shout encouragement to the last competitors to finish. I don't think anyone had either the energy to go over to another lane or enough in his lungs to voice more than a few grunts.

As miserable of a workout as that was for me, I still placed fifth. Matt won the event, but he was the only one among those closest to me in the overall standings who finished ahead of me.

Moving Closer

The next event, held three hours later back inside the tennis stadium, was a fun event for me. The clean ladder is one clean every thirty seconds, beginning at 245 pounds and increasing by 10 pounds each rep. A failed rep ends your progression up the ladder. For this event, there was an extra wrinkle, as after you failed on a clean, you had to deadlift that bar as many times as possible before the thirty seconds ran out. The number of deadlifts you did would serve as the tiebreaker in case of a tie on the clean weight.

As the overall leader, I was the last man to start the

clean ladder. Neal Maddox had turned in the highest rep at 365 pounds, and I had my sights set on that number when I left the second row of weights for the third row, which began at 345. I made the first lift there, and I was pumped up when I slammed the weight back to the floor. But the 355-pound bar got me, and I had to settle for fifth place. Again, though, I was at least able to place more distance between me and my closest competitors.

Saturday's final event was called Chipper—a name you can apply to any series of movements that you "chip away" at. The movements were 10 overhead squats (155 pounds), 10 twenty-four-inch box jump-overs, 10 fat-bar thrusters (135 pounds), 10 power cleans (205 pounds), 10 toes-to-bar, 10 burpee muscle-ups, and then reversing back through each movement to end with the overhead squats.

We were in twelve-man heats, so I could keep an eye on all the competitors within striking distance of my lead. Chipper was one of those events where it took a while for the pack to begin to sort itself out, but when we started back through the second half of the workout, I was the first one out of the toes-to-bar with Matt Chan not far behind me in the third lane.

I was facing Matt on the power cleans and could tell I had a bit of a quicker pace than he did. That gave me a touch more of a lead going into the thrusters, and I knew all I had to do was stay ahead of Matt and I'd be okay for the rest of that event. I still hadn't won an event, and I really wanted to win this one.

During the box jump-overs, I kept watching Matt. Jason Khalipa had made up good ground halfway across the floor, but I still held a decent lead. By the time I got back to the overhead squats, I knew I would win the heat, but I didn't know how my time would compare to the first two heats.

Thankfully, it compared well. I finally—finally!—had won an event. What a weight off my shoulders. I knew my overall lead was growing, and I was confident in how the weekend was going, but I hadn't liked the possibility that I could win the Games—become the first back-to-back champion—without winning a single event. This may sound difficult to believe, but that could have put a damper on winning the title.

However, I didn't have to worry about that anymore when I went back to the hotel Saturday night leading Matt 740 to 652. Kyle Kasperbauer was in third with 609 points.

There would be four events on Sunday, including the customary three-event finale. The first event was Double Banger. A banger, as it turned out, was exactly that. We had to take a sledgehammer and bang a heavy weight across a sliding track. Actually we had to bang three weights—one on a low track, one where we had to stand straddling the weight and hit it by swinging the hammer down between our legs, and one on a waist-high track. (Maybe they should have called it Triple Banger.) Before each banger we had to do 50 double-unders.

Double Banger seemed to be the crowd's favorite event that weekend. Perhaps it's because when we were doing the bangers, it looked like we were on a construction job. Just another day on Mom and Dad's land doing some work!

I had aimed to come out and pretty much put things away with the first event of the day. I couldn't clinch the championship that early, but I wanted to start the final day with a strong performance, finish ahead of the two or three closest to me, and put more distance between us. I wanted to send a message that I wasn't going to have a bad day and, as much as possible early in the final day, wipe out anyone else's thoughts that they would be able to overtake me.

But Double Banger proved to be my most frustrating event of that year's Games. Nobody is going to run away from the rest of the guys in the heat in a short workout like Double Banger, and as expected, it was a close race two-thirds of the way through. By the third set of double-unders, I wasn't out front, but I was right there among the leaders. But when I finished the double-unders and tossed my jump rope aside, the judge told me I had not completed the required fifty. By my count, I had done more than fifty, but we had a different count. I had to go pick up my rope and finish the set, and that cost me several seconds.

In an event where the winning time would be less than three minutes, those extra seconds that far into the workout eliminated any chance of winning the heat. I finished ninth overall and gave back a couple of points to Matt, who was eighth, and a bunch of points to Kyle, who won the event and the 100 points.

We had about three hours until our final trio of events when Jeff Barnett, my mathematician, called me with an update.

"You want to know what you need to do?" he asked.

"Tell me," I said.

"Win one event and it's over."

THRUSTER
Holding a barbell in front of you in rack position, go into a full squat, then simultaneously stand and thrust the barbell overhead.

///

Bringing It Home

The first event of the three-event finale would be the benchmark workout Elizabeth: 21-15-9 reps, for time, of cleans (135 pounds) and ring dips. I expected that to be a good event for me. With the field cut to eighteen, there would be three heats, and all eighteen of us would be on the floor together watching each other's heats. Going into our final heat, I knew the time to beat was the 2:43 posted by Austin Malleolo.

I was in lane one with my back to the other competitors, so I couldn't see how anyone else was doing until I was done with my first set of cleans. Things were pretty tight at that point, and as I finished with the 21 ring dips, Kyle Kasperbauer was slightly ahead of me. Then, on my second rep in the second set of cleans, the judge called a no-rep. I didn't have my elbows far enough forward after I brought the bar up to my chest. I didn't let it faze me; I just kept going. By the time I was finished with that set, I was the leader.

Halfway through the third set, when I left the cleans for the ring dips and my final 9 reps, I took a quick look at all the lanes to my left and saw that I was the only one finished with the cleans. I knew I had the heat won—it was just a matter of beating Austin's time. I touched down from my final ring dip and looked up to the scoreboard to see my time of 2:33. I knew what that meant. I clenched both fists and let out about as loud of a yell as I'll let out during a competition. I looked to the far side of the stadium, where my family and friends were sitting, and pointed toward them. It wasn't official, but I knew as long as I stayed in for the final two events, I was going to be the back-to-back CrossFit Games champion.

Here is what went through my mind at that moment, knowing that, for all intents and purposes, I had wrapped up my second consecutive Games title: *Bring on Isabel!*

Isabel, the second workout of the finale, is another CrossFit classic—30 snatches for time at 135 pounds. It's short and brutal, and I was looking forward to it.

This might sound bad, and I certainly don't mean it in a negative way, but I wanted to score as many points as I could. I didn't want to run up the score on anyone, though the competitor in me did want to win by as many points as possible.

An extra motivation came when I looked at the packed stadium. The crowds had been great—big and loud all weekend—and I wanted to put on a show for them. And in the process, I wanted to prove that I deserved to be the champion. I didn't want anyone leaving the stadium saying, "That Froning shouldn't have won."

I wanted to leave no doubt.

I wanted to complete all 30 snatches unbroken, but I had to drop the bar after rep 20 and again after 25. I felt my legs turning to Jell-O as I struggled to lift the 135 pounds above my head for the twenty-ninth time, but there was absolutely no way I was going to drop the bar, walk away, and have to regroup for number 30. I was finishing that bad boy off right then and there. And when I locked my arms above my head for the final time, I held my pose a little bit longer than normal.

I had won Isabel by more than four seconds with a time of 1:20.7—and I broke my personal record for the workout in the process.

No doubt.

No more left in the tank, either.

Fran was our final workout: 21-15-9 reps of thrusters (95 pounds) and pull-ups.

There was no winning Fran. It wasn't an event I could have won under ordinary circumstances, and I sure wasn't going to win it after going all out for Elizabeth and Isabel.

Just get through this one, and then it's all over, I coached myself.

I placed fifth in Fran to officially finish first in the Games for the second consecutive year. Matt Chan was second overall, and Kyle Kasperbauer was third. My great friend, workout partner, and convenient scapegoat at home, Dan Bailey, came in sixth for the second consecutive year.

Iceland Annie

I would be remiss if I didn't say that the way the schedule worked out, I was not the first back-to-back champion in the history of the CrossFit Games. I was the first men's back-to-back champ. The women's final event was held before ours, and Annie Thorisdottir won the women's title for the second consecutive year.

Annie, who is from Iceland, is the most competitive person I've ever known. Male or female. Hands down. She could have been one of my cousins, and there aren't many people I would say that about. She is so competitive that when we've appeared at CrossFit demonstrations together, she'd say quietly to me, "We're gonna go at like 70 percent on this, right?" I'd agree with her, and then she'd start right out going 100 percent, and I'd have to bust it to catch up to her. Annie can turn a friendly demonstration into an all-out war. That's competitive.

Annie is dedicated to her workouts and trains seriously hard, so I was glad to see her become a repeat champion too.

/// CROSSFIT DEFINED //////////////////////////////////////

RING DIP

A dip executed on gymnastic rings. To perform a dip, support yourself above rings or parallel bars, then bend your elbows and lower your body as far as you can before pushing yourself back up. For ring dips, the CrossFit standard is that in the bottom position, your biceps have to touch the tops of the rings, and in the top position, your elbows have to be completely locked.

//

A Tough Loss

When I met up with my family and friends after the medal ceremony, I couldn't resist thinking back to this same meeting after the previous two Games.

"Hey, Hillary, you hungry again?"

Hillary's awesome. It's really not important to her where I finish. She watches and she gets concerned that I might injure myself and she roots for me to do well. But as soon as the Games are over, they're over. Where I place carries no significance for what she thinks of me.

Hillary's dad, Bill, was a Division I quarterback, and her sister, Ali, signed to play basketball at Charleston Southern University. Hillary's a decent athlete too, but she's just not competitive in sports. She's tried CrossFit a couple of times and made it about two weeks each time before deciding it wasn't her thing.

There was one day I came home after having a great day at the gym, and she told me, "I watched this video of you doing this workout, and there's all these comments on Facebook about how crazy it was that you did it. I don't get it. It's just not impressive to me."

"Thanks, Hill."

But that's good for me. She's perfect for me because she keeps balance in my life. Some nights, she'll declare a no-CrossFit-talk rule around the house with Dan and me. I could easily overload on CrossFit if it weren't for Hillary helping keep me in check.

After I won in 2012 and, yes, Hillary answered that she was hungry, we went out to eat with our family and some friends. That's where the newly crowned two-time CrossFit Games champion—the Fittest Man on Earth—got into big trouble. I received a dose of humble pie before any desserts were ordered.

At dinner I was talking and motioning with my hands. Hillary noticed my bare ring finger.

"Where's your wedding band?" she interrupted.

Before the ball toss and track triplet on Friday, I had taken off my watch and put my wedding band on the watch strap. I secured the watch strap and handed my watch and ring to Darren for him to keep.

After the triplet, I asked Darren, "Where's my watch and wedding band?"

"What wedding band?" he asked.

"It was on my watch," I told him.

Darren had put my watch on his wrist so he wouldn't have to carry it. He didn't know my band was on the strap and it fell off. Where it fell, we never found out.

No one other than Darren and my dad knew the band was lost; I had wanted to wait until Hillary and I were alone to tell her. But our family and friends were divided up into men's and women's rooms at the Games hotel, so I hadn't had a chance to tell Hillary.

When Hillary asked her question at dinner, I had to fess up in front of everyone, and she was none too pleased I had lost my ring.

I couldn't put this one on Dan. And even though I tried, I wasn't successful at pinning the blame on Darren, either.

My crazy dad had been trying to find me a replacement band before Hillary found out, although I promise that if he had found one, I would have told her anyway. I ordered a new ring immediately the next day and, based on the grand lesson learned, thought up a new rule for future Games: I will either give my wedding band to Hillary when I compete or make 100 percent certain the person I hand my watch to knows the ring is on the strap.

After the hot water I got into at the restaurant had cooled off, we headed back to the hotel, where there was a humongous post-Games party. I'm not a fan of crowds, and I could anticipate how it might be for the now-two-time champion when I showed up at the hotel, especially with the party already nearing full speed.

I wanted to go to my room first before coming back down to the party, but we all were concerned about my ability to get through the lobby and to the elevators without being noticed. That's when my bodyguards sprang into action. Yes, I had two bodyguards. One was Hillary's cousin Dusty Hill, who weighs 120 pounds. The other was a friend, Justin Morgan, who is a cross-country runner. You know how cross-country runners are built. Justin would have to be soaking wet to get the scales to 120 pounds. But somehow, with my large bodyguards running interference, I made it to the elevator undetected.

I didn't make it to the party. The more I thought about

going, the more I thought about how many people were down there. Put more than fifteen people in a fairly small room and I start to freak out. I couldn't imagine how I would have handled a large banquet room filled with people. I felt bad for not going, but with that size crowd, I just couldn't do it.

So that's how the two-time champion and his family celebrated that evening: dinner and a quiet night in our hotel rooms.

Hillary and I stayed in Los Angeles with our families for a day, and then we went to Laguna Beach for three days. We had wanted to find a place to surf but instead just kind of chilled out.

And there even was one day while we were there that I didn't work out.

CHAPTER 18

WINNING WITH THE MIND

THERE ARE, WITHOUT DOUBT, thousands of people in the world who are more physically talented than I am. If we were to compare ourselves in general physical skills, there are people who would probably beat me in all of them. That is the main reason I work out so much, going back to the days of having the dirtiest uniform on my baseball teams. For me to be successful, I cannot allow anyone to outwork me.

So where are those thousands I know have me beat physically? That's a good question that digs to the very core of CrossFit. As a coach and an athlete, I've observed countless people whose bodies have more to give them, but their minds tell them they can go no further, and they listen to their minds.

The human body is an incredible machine, but most people only get out of that machine what their mind allows them to.

Athletes at the CrossFit Games train all year for one weekend of competition, and the ones who make it to California are the ones who not only have trained their bodies to perform at the highest levels but also have trained their minds to the highest levels.

It's that mental part that is the most difficult to train for, but it's the most important. I believe the Games are 70 percent mental and 30 percent physical.

Secrets to Success

The physical volume and intensity of my workouts have received a lot of press. From the Games through the end of the calendar year, I mostly follow my body's lead with my workouts. Usually that means a couple of workouts per day, every day. A morning session will last an hour to two hours, depending on the workout I choose. About midday, I'll come back with another one- to two-hour workout. I'm not going full speed the entire time. In a two-hour workout, for example, I'm not doing two hours of as many rounds as possible. I'll take short breaks in between the various movements, check my e-mails and texts, do a short interview, or play with my black Lab, Gilligan. (Gilligan enjoys being at the gym as much as I do.)

I listen to my body. If my body needs a rest, I'll work out

just once. If a certain part of my body feels tired, I'll design a workout so that part can basically have a day off.

But real soon after the first of the year, something in my head will click, and I'll start ramping up my training. I can't explain how my mind seems to know when it's time. It's just that I've had a few months to hang out and enjoy myself, but my mind will decide it's time to get down to business.

I'll continue to make appearances on behalf of my sponsors and film video interviews for CrossFit HQ after the new year begins, but I'm more schedule-conscious with the business side of being an athlete so that nothing sidetracks my preparation. If an event does cause me to miss a workout, I'll think, *Oh, tomorrow you're going to pay for that.* I know that despite my best efforts, there will be things that pop up and impact my training. Illness, an item on the schedule not going as planned, whatever. When that happens, I stay determined mentally to get back into my workouts and limit the damage.

During January, leading up to the Open, is when it becomes "Go Time." After the Open, starting about eight weeks out from Regionals, it's "Really Go Time." It's almost like when Dave Castro says, "Three, two, one, go!" to start an event at the Games and that tunnel vision kicks in. I shift into full-on preparation. Anything that is not directly part of training for the Games does not find a place on my schedule. There are smart people at our gym to handle the gym's business.

I'll work out up to five times a day, seven days a week during my "Really Go Time." My programming schedule isn't rigid, but I try to do Olympic lifting five days a week and metabolic conditioning six days a week. *Metcon* is the CrossFit term for metabolic conditioning. Without getting too scientific, metcon workouts consist of highly functional movements executed at highly intense rates. Metcons last anywhere from two to thirty minutes, and because they get the heart rate up, they are great for the cardiovascular system.

I employ a reward philosophy in my workouts. To push myself to train on the movements I don't like, I'll reward myself for doing them by following up with movements I do like. I've made abundantly clear my strong dislike for running. I like Olympic lifting just as much as I dislike running. So I'll schedule a running workout before an Olympic lifting workout. Knowing that I'll soon be lifting helps me make it through the running.

The real secret to my success, though, is my workout partners. I always surround myself with people who are better than me or will push me.

Dan Bailey is a part of that, although we don't work out together as much as most people assume, especially in the final few months leading up to the Games. Even after the 2012 Games, we haven't trained together as much as we did previously. It's not anything we discussed and decided to do, and it's not because there's any awkwardness with us being competitors as well as friends. It started because we both got busy with our own schedules, with Dan working at Tennessee Tech and me working at my gym. As a result, we started working out at our own times.

Just to be clear so no rumors are started by people trying to read between the lines, there are no problems between Dan and me. Everything is as fine as it's always been. I still have to pick up after him around the house, but I also get to blame him for whatever trouble I get myself into. So nothing has changed!

I have intentionally selected workout partners who aren't caught up in that "Rich Froning the CrossFitter" hype. My cousin Darren, Thomas Cox, and Donovan Degrie push me and don't cut me any slack. I don't want people around me who will say, "Oh, you're tired today? Well, you're the two-time-defending CrossFit Games champion, so go ahead and skip a workout. You've earned it."

On days when I'm not motivated like I need to be, Darren, Thomas, or Donovan will say, "You don't feel like doing anything today? Too bad. We're going to do this." They've pushed me to the success I've had in CrossFit, and I'll need them to continue to push me if I'm going to continue to be successful.

I also have purposefully not selected workout partners whom I can beat all the time. Darren has competed at Regionals with the CrossFit Faith team, and I think he has what it takes physically to compete as an individual at the Games if he wanted to. Darren's strength is in endurance, and he pushes me to get better so that I can keep up with him on long workouts. Thomas also competes with CrossFit Faith, and he beats me in some of the strength events or heavier lifts.

Balancing Act

I'm a sore loser. I don't like losing events at the Games, so it can be a kick to the ego to be outdone by a friend or a trash-talking cousin in my gym or in my own garage. But he who beats me in my gym or garage makes me better in the Games. Besides, I remind them, they each can beat me in different things, but it's only in those areas that they're better than me. Take everything into account and, hey, I'm not above laying the *I'm the champ* card on the table in front of them when I need to!

Balance is the key to the Games.

I'm not saying I could reach a point where I could destroy Darren in every endurance workout, but if I made that my goal and worked to achieve it, that could wind up costing me a championship. When you hyperfocus on one area, other areas will suffer.

Here's an example. Other than winning the Games again, there is nothing I would like to accomplish more than winning a running event. They're not terrible events for me, but I hate them. My favorite workout is Amanda, a 9-7-5 combo of muscle-ups and 135-pound snatches. My least favorite workout is any that includes running.

I've had to push myself to run in my training. Running isn't exactly a weakness because I can hold my own in running events. (I finished fourth in the track triplet in 2012.) If it were a weakness, it would be automatic that I'd have to train for it more. But because it's not a weakness, it's a struggle to keep myself motivated—such as with the reward system—to run as much as I need to.

As a result, winning a running event would be a big deal to me. And I think I could probably improve my running enough to where I would have a serious shot at winning the right event. But more than likely, that would cost me points in other events. The time I would spend running would have to come out of the time I spend training in other areas. So as much as I'd like to win a running event—and if I ever do, there might be a celebration—I have to keep my ego in check and keep the big picture in mind.

There is no room for specialization in the Games. There's an art to finding the right balance that allows you to compete the best across the board, because becoming really good in one area can cause you to become deficient in another. It's also possible to overimprove an area in which you are already good. That comes into play often because we all are trying to get better.

For me, increased strength has been one of my focuses since my first Games, but increased strength puts more weight on me, and increased weight affects the gymnastics movements like handstands, push-ups, pull-ups, and muscle-ups.

Finding and then maintaining balance is a constant battle, and that's part of what makes CrossFit fun. There always is something to work on, yet there always is a cost to consider for becoming better in a particular area.

That's why I think it is impossible for someone to win every event.

How to Get Better at CrossFit

To me, the best way to get better at CrossFit is by doing CrossFit. It's that simple. That said, there are specific training techniques that can help a lot.

There are two things I do not do in preparing for the Games: one, put too much stock into what other competitors are doing in their workouts; and two, try to read Dave Castro's mind.

I don't scout other competitors. Part of CrossFit HQ's job between Games is to keep things interesting for CrossFit fans. Thus, there will be reports about this person improving in this area or that person looking good in that area, but I don't pay any attention to them.

As for trying to read Dave's mind . . . no thanks. Dave Castro and Tony Budding, the codirectors of the CrossFit Games, are the villains responsible for creating the events each year. That has to be a fun job—I'd like the opportunity one day to help determine the workouts. I'm sure there is a much deeper process than there appears to be that goes into selecting the workouts, and I'm fairly sure there isn't as much evil scheming that goes into it as I sometimes think there is.

I've been asked if I have spotted trends in the Games workouts. I have not. And if I were to detect trends, I don't know that I would change anything about my preparation anyway. Dave is so smart that I would be concerned he was allowing us to see a trend to set us up for a complete trend-buster the next time we showed up to compete. But I've seen no trends. In my three Games, we have been assigned just about everything that could possibly be thought of. So there are no attempts at predicting events.

Dave usually isn't going to throw something off-the-wall at us that we haven't done in some way, shape, or form—in general, the workouts are going to be variations of standard CrossFit movements. He may come up with slightly altered versions of handstand push-ups or the clean or the snatch, but the best way to prepare for the possible variations is to be fluent in all the CrossFit movements. Remember, in the Games you need to be prepared for anything—the unknown and unknowable. So why bother trying to figure anything out ahead of time?

My workout partners and I sometimes make up and compete in workouts that we think could be Games events, but there is no way to know what's going on inside Dave's mind. He's a former Navy SEAL, and he doesn't let too many people in on his thought process.

One key to proper preparation is variety. By coming up with as many different variations in training as possible, the hope is that no matter what movements may be sprung on us at the Games, I'll be able to tell myself, *I've done this before. I remember doing this.* I may not be the best at that movement, but at least I'll have some experience with it. Experience is an important factor in avoiding that one bomb that can't be afforded at a Games. Besides, the calm of the gym is the best place to learn a new movement or a variation.

I tried to learn the rope climb on the fly in 2010, and we all know how that turned out.

But no matter how good you are at coming up with new variations, there's no replicating the Games in training. I could do a workout in my Cookeville gym and then do the exact same thing in front of a packed house at the Home Depot Center, and it would feel completely different.

The speed of workouts feels so much faster during the Games than elsewhere because of the energy from the crowd, going head-to-head with the other competitors, and the nervous anticipation I feel before events. It's just a totally different experience that is difficult to adequately prepare for until you've been through it.

My Curious Diet

If there's anything that stirs up questions about my Games preparation as much as my volume of workouts, it's my diet. Or lack thereof.

I don't have any serious diet restrictions, and I don't count calories. (I also do not keep up with how many calories I burn.) Just like with my workouts, my body tells me what I need to know. I follow the *Forrest Gump* diet plan: when I'm hungry, I eat; when I'm thirsty, I drink.

For breakfast, I typically have a protein shake because it's quick and easy. (Though Dan can make a tasty breakfast, and I'll consider making an exception when he's cooking.) Sleep is important for my physical recovery, and when the Games are getting near, I try to get to bed around 9 or 10 p.m. and to sleep in until about 9 a.m. I'm not always successful on both ends of that time range, but I try. Because I prefer to sleep in, a protein shake enables me to get out of the house and to my first workout quicker. Shakes don't sit heavy in my stomach, and that makes it possible to work out immediately after drinking one.

I don't have a sit-down lunch most days. My parents were the same way, so I must have picked that up from them. Mom and Dad would get going on their projects in the morning and eat a snack or something light and quick around lunchtime in order to keep the projects moving. For the most part, I don't get hungry during the day. When I do, I'll eat a spoonful or two of peanut butter for an energy boost.

At night is when I eat my only true meal of the day. My food choice then is whatever's for dinner.

I avoid pasta—which is Hillary's favorite type of food—because I don't like the way I feel after eating it. I will eat pizza, but only thin crust. I'm not a big fan of bread and rice, though I do get on kicks where I like eating bread, so I can be hit-or-miss on leaving bread out of my diet. When I'm being good, I'll order burgers without the buns. But I can eat a good old fried Southern meal and not feel guilty. During "Really Go Time," I do try to make smarter choices.

Some days I'm hungrier than others, and I've yet to figure out what makes the difference from one day to the next. I've also noticed that when I'm sitting around and bored, I tend to be hungrier. I think my body feeds off whatever I'm doing.

I'm a big milk drinker. I love whole milk, especially before and after workouts, and I'll typically drink half to three-quarters of a gallon per day. After a workout, I like to add a BSN nutritional supplement to a glass of chocolate milk. I'll occasionally drink a diet pop, but for the most part it's whole milk and water for me.

There is one weakness in my diet I have yet to attack: my sweet tooth. I'm willing to accept that as a weakness and leave it be. Actually, I tend to feed that weakness, if you know what I mean.

My mom is an absolutely incredible baker of desserts. When I was growing up, there always was something sweet to eat in the house. She has a long list of specialties, but one of my favorites is a dessert pizza made with croissants, granola, and fruit.

Mom's desserts are worth the extra reps in the gym.

CHAPTER 19

KEEPING OUR SPORT CLEAN

The list of sports that haven't been touched by scandals involving performance-enhancing drugs is a short one.

As more and more people get interested in CrossFit competitions and as the prize dollars and publicity increase for those who are at the top of the sport, I hope our sport can stay on that short list. I know HQ takes the issue of PEDs seriously.

I've been tested at every Regionals and Games. In each of the Games divisions (men, women, teams, and the Masters age groups), each person who makes the podium plus others selected at random must submit to drug tests. I heard that more than a hundred drug tests were administered throughout the weekend at the 2012 Games.

In this era of athletes cheating to gain any advantage possible, I appreciate being confident that we compete on a level playing field. I want HQ to do whatever it takes to keep it that way too.

Discussions about PEDs focus so much on the cheating aspect that the health risks tend to get overlooked. All of us as sports fans have observed the athletes who have paid the penalty with their bodies, and sometimes their lives, for using PEDs. I have a feeling that we're going to see a significant increase in those cases over the next several years as the negative effects of the more widespread use of PEDs start to take their tolls on former athletes' bodies.

Also, it isn't just me as an athlete who depends on HQ to discourage cheating. CrossFit is my full-time job. The money that I am making in and through CrossFit is what is going to provide for Hillary, me, and the kids we plan to have. I don't think the average fan realizes how much everyone who competes in a sport, plus their families, has at stake when it comes to PEDs.

I admit that I might be naive on this, but I just don't see how steroids, for example, would actually enhance performance in CrossFit. I would be concerned that steroid use would make someone too strong or bulky and disrupt that delicate balance I talked about in the previous chapter. Blood doping and human growth hormones might be a different story. I haven't researched them, but from the knowledge I have picked up, I suppose there could be ways those might help someone who competes at the Games level.

What I know for sure is that I won't be using them. The main reason, plain and simple, is that it's not the right thing to do. That's not even a negotiable with me. Second, I'm not going to be conducting any experiments with my body. When I had the back injury, I didn't even want to fill any of the prescriptions the doctor gave me for the pain.

I'm still impacted by the talk my dad gave me when I was in high school.

"All right," he said. "You're a heck of an athlete. I don't want to see you throw it away. You've got possibilities of going to play college ball."

Oh, man, I thought. *Here comes the birds and the bees talk.*

"And I can't tell you," my dad said, "what you can and can't do because you're gonna do it anyway if you want to."

Here we go.

"I don't recommend smoking weed or doing any drugs."

That wasn't what I was expecting.

"Because I did when I was in high school. And it made me lazy. I was an athlete, and it made me not want to do anything."

That decided it for me. I don't think Dad could have given me a more effective antidrug speech. At the time, I really wanted to be a professional baseball player. I knew the odds of making it were steep to begin with, and I did not want to do anything that would reduce my chances. I've never touched any illegal drugs and have never even wanted to. I've had friends who have had their sports careers and their occupations end early because of drug and alcohol abuse. It's sad to look back and see what they had the potential to become, and I've never wanted to risk becoming that type of story.

I know there are people on the CrossFit message boards who are vocal with their suspicions that I could not win the Games while clean. Among the things I cannot do to change their minds is getting on the message boards and answering their charges. That would be fruitless. I compete in an era of sports where suspicion comes almost by default. I understand why, too, with all the star athletes who have admitted to using PEDs, and even more so because of the star athletes who denied using PEDs but later were proved to be lying.

That makes me wonder if it's worth stating in interviews and even here in my own book that I have never used PEDs. From my experience, those who believe athletes who say that already believe those athletes are clean and don't need to hear them say that they are. Those who are suspicious are going to remain suspicious regardless of who claims what and how many times or with how much passion they say it.

Since I've started competing in the Games, I've gained a different perspective on the PEDs discussions. Before, I was among the cynical. I'd see an athlete perform at the top of his sport and think, *He's got to be doing something.*

But now I've gone over to the other side—the side that used to be the starting point for these discussions—that says people are innocent until proven guilty. If there comes a time when they're proven guilty, they're guilty and deserve whatever sanctions their sports call for. But until then, I think they deserve my respect for their athletic abilities. I've learned what it takes to compete and succeed in a sport, and all the suspicion that is in place now in the sports world seems to negate the hard work of athletes. Now I can relate because I know how it feels to be accused by people who have no idea what they're talking about yet talk loudly anyway, even in the face of repeated drug tests that counter their claims.

While we're on this topic, I'd like to briefly share advice concerning nutrition supplements. I have an endorsement contract with BSN, and I regularly use BSN supplements. I take protein, fish oil, and amino acids, which are proteins that have been broken down. Every once in a while, when my body feels beat up, I take creatine. Most of the supplements I take are for recovery. I don't take anything preworkout or to get jacked up for a workout.

I want to offer this caution for anyone taking or considering supplements: do your homework. Part of the education CrossFit provides athletes regarding supplements includes an International Olympic Committee analysis of several hundred supplements; the study found that almost 15 percent of them contain substances that not only aren't listed on the product label but also would cause an athlete to fail a drug test. In addition, 19 percent of seemingly legal supplements in the United States were tainted with banned substances.

CrossFit puts the responsibility on athletes. We are entirely accountable for what we put into our bodies. I recommend that each of you accept the same responsibility. Don't just go by what a label says. Check the reputation of those who sell you supplements. Unfortunately retailers can be misinformed or deceitful. Some can be both. Read up on the company that manufactures the product before you make a single purchase. Buy supplements that are as all-natural as possible. The fewer additives and sugar they contain, the better they are for you.

You may not be competing and may not have to be concerned about tests for performance enhancers, but there are great reasons beyond competitive ones why banned substances are banned.

There are plenty of safe products out there to help you improve your fitness. Please take the steps necessary to make sure that those are the ones you put into your body because, after all, it is *your* body. What a shame it would be to severely damage your body—and perhaps even forfeit your life—all in the name of getting fit.

CHAPTER 20

A GYM WITH A PURPOSE

AFTER THE 2012 GAMES, Hillary and I made a trip to Michigan to visit family. The comparisons still go on between the cousins, but my being the two-time Games champion has proved to be (in my opinion) too much for the others to top.

Another round of King of the Dock broke out on our visit. There were about twenty of us playing—so many that when the dock got loaded, it would actually be a little bit underwater. Of course, everyone was ganging up on me because they all wanted to boast that they had pushed the Fittest Man on Earth off the dock. It was mass chaos.

The game was easier to play when I was younger. I remember playing King of the Dock back in the old days against uncles who were about ten years older. They were still young enough to play with us, but as we cousins became older, the uncles seemed to grow softer. Now I can understand why. Even though I'm only twenty-five, I can already notice how my flexibility isn't what it was when I was a youngster. Those little aches seem to linger a bit longer now, such as the thumb I twisted when I fell off the dock. It was killing me for two weeks afterward.

I must be getting soft in my old age too, because I was more willing to cede my spot on the dock the last time we played than I used to be.

CrossFit Invitational

In October 2012, I had the honor of taking part in the first CrossFit Invitational, a Team USA vs. Team Europe competition held in London and broadcast on live television in Europe. The event drew a sellout crowd of about two thousand people to the ExCeL Centre, which was one of the venues for the 2012 Olympic Games.

It was cool to compete in an Olympic arena, and it was an awesome experience to represent the United States. My dad's always been patriotic and supportive of the military, so I grew up respecting the American flag and what it stands for.

The team format also allowed me to compete on the same team with women and men I respect—Kristan Clever, Julie Foucher, Rebecca Voigt, Matt Chan, and Jason Khalipa. Again, it was almost a pinch-myself moment being teammates with athletes I had watched on CrossFit videos before I started competing. Not only that, but I was asked to serve as our team captain.

The Invitational was designed to be a fun showcase, but the athletes' competitive natures came out as early as the pre-Invitational meeting when the teams got together to select the workouts. That meeting got a little edgy because both sides were trying to angle selections so the workouts would favor them. So it got kind of serious.

The competition consisted of four stages. The first three stages were comprised of three events each, and the fourth was a one-event finale. Each event was worth either two or three points to the winning team, except for the six-point finale. It was close at first, with Team USA holding a 7 to 6 lead after the first two stages. Then we swept the three events in Stage 3 to take a 14 to 6 lead. With six points at stake in the last event, we had already clinched a win. But we continued working hard and won the finale, too, to finish with a 20 to 6 victory.

It was a fun event but turned out to be extremely competitive, too. Everyone was aware that they were representing their home country, and so there was that element of pride that came into play. From a competitive standpoint, I'd say it was on par with the Games, but I wouldn't attempt to make the two events equal because the Invitational took place within an entirely different dynamic.

The biggest difference was, because it was a made-for-TV event, it lasted only an hour and a half. It was short, and that made it difficult to get into a groove as an athlete, but it was a lot of fun to participate. Plus, Team USA won!

Pure Mayhem

The biggest event for me following the 2012 Games came when our CrossFit Mayhem gym held its grand opening in early December.

CrossFit Mayhem has a short but interesting history. It began in Dad's barn with Darren and me training a few clients in 2009. Then we were able to use the free space in a friend's gymnastics and cheerleading studio. At that time we had the name Power Fitness Gym. After Dave Castro made it possible for us to become a CrossFit affiliate, we changed the name to CrossFit Mayhem.

The Mayhem name goes back to my cousin Donnie. When we were trying to come up with a good name for the gym, one of the cousins brought up Project Mayhem from Donnie's favorite movie, *Fight Club*. As soon as we heard *mayhem*, we knew that was our name.

Shortly after becoming an affiliate in May 2010, we moved into a bigger location. The following January was when I went to work for Chip Pugh at Tennessee Tech. Chip ran an affiliate called CrossFit Cookeville out of Tennessee Tech's weight room. Now, not only did I have CrossFit Mayhem to operate with Darren, but I also worked with Chip's CrossFit, plus I had my coach's job at Tech. That quickly got to be too much, and Chip and I worked out a merger of sorts. CrossFit

Mayhem closed down in March 2011, and Darren and I worked at CrossFit Cookeville.

That arrangement went on for about a year. After I signed with BSN and resigned from my job at Tech, I continued working at CrossFit Cookeville. Before I left Tech, the school had opened a brand-new athletic performance center. It was a sweet facility with top-of-the-line equipment, and as a service to the community, the school allowed CrossFit Cookeville to continue operating out of that facility. The problem was that there was limited time when the APC wasn't being used by the school's athletes. As a result, the only CrossFit class was at 6 p.m. With CrossFit becoming more popular, the demand far outweighed the supply.

After the 2011 Regionals, Chip came to me and said there was no room for CrossFit Cookeville to grow at Tech because the athletes had to be given first priority. Plus, since the time when Chip had started teaching CrossFit about four years earlier, he and his wife, Nicole, had had two daughters.

"I'm going to close down CrossFit Cookeville," he told me.

I decided it was time to reopen CrossFit Mayhem.

The owner of Rogue Fitness, which is the official equipment supplier for the CrossFit Games, is a guy named Bill Henniger. When I told Bill I was planning to reopen my own CrossFit facility, he made me an amazing offer. He said that as part of my endorsement contract with Rogue, his company would supply all the equipment for our gym. Stunned and grateful, I didn't know what to say. It was just like when Dave Castro offered to waive the first year's affiliate fee for me back at the 2010 Regionals. I still can hardly believe Bill's generosity when I walk into the gym and see all the equipment being used by our members.

We signed a lease on a building in August 2012, and in September CrossFit Cookeville officially became CrossFit Mayhem. We started training clients in our work-in-progress gym but didn't hold our official grand opening until December. Dan Bailey, who is one of our six coaches, and I signed autographs for the grand opening. Our coaches put on CrossFit demonstrations and led people through workouts to introduce them to CrossFit. We wanted to make the event about more than just our gym, so with Christmas coming up, we asked people to provide a donation to Toys for Tots as their entry fee.

We had a great turnout. CrossFit HQ was there to take video footage of the grand opening. I met one guy who drove seven hours to attend. I also met a family of four who drove in from West Virginia. All four were CrossFitters and wanted to work out in our gym. That family also presented me with the strangest autograph request I've ever received.

"Will you sign my forehead?" the twelve-year-old boy asked.

"Not unless your mom says it's okay," I replied.

"He's fine," the mother said.

I thought the mother meant that he was fine without having his head signed, so I started signing for other people.

As the family was walking away, I heard the mom ask her son, "Did you get your forehead signed?"

"It's okay?" I asked her.

"It's fine," she said.

"All right," I said and signed the boy's forehead. Hopefully my signature didn't stay there long.

Our gym has more than one hundred members now, and it's still growing. That's exciting because the reason CrossFit Mayhem exists is not to be a place where I can prepare for CrossFit competitions. It is a place where I can observe what CrossFit truly is.

CrossFit isn't about the Games. It's not about the six hundred or so people competing in front of a sold-out crowd at the Home Depot Center and in front of a worldwide television and Internet audience. CrossFit is about being fit. It's about the thousands and thousands of people who faithfully walk into their local gym either before or after work because they want to be fit and healthy.

Too many CrossFitters get caught up in doing CrossFit so they can one day compete in the Games. Sorry, but that's not going to happen for the large majority. Especially with the way CrossFit keeps growing worldwide, the chances of an individual making it to the Games are dropping. Who knows—ten years from now, the pool of competitors could be so large and advanced that it might be next to impossible for some guy working out with his cousin inside his dad's barn to make it to the next year's Games.

The Games get a lot of attention, but all they really are is an advertisement for CrossFit. The Games didn't make CrossFit; CrossFit made the Games.

I'm blessed to have our CrossFit Mayhem gym, where I can see the daily reminders of what CrossFit truly is and who CrossFit is for.

Gilligan and I spend as much time in the gym as we can. The gym is a good place for me because it's a place where I can be "just Rich."

It's also a place for my family.

Hillary is a dental assistant, and she and her sister also manage fifteen properties they inherited. But Hillary puts in extra time helping out with some of the business side of the gym. My mom works out there. My dad, not surprisingly, takes care of projects around the gym, building anything we need or fixing anything that breaks. "I don't need to do CrossFit," he tells me. "I do *real* work."

One of my two main priorities with CrossFit Mayhem is setting up Hillary and me for the future. I want to make enough money with the gym that Hillary doesn't have to work if she doesn't want to. When we have kids and if she decides she wants to stay home with them, I want her to be able to do that.

My other priority concerns my cousin Darren, who is one of the coaches and one of my workout partners.

Darren's my little brother now. I didn't have a brother growing up, and nothing against my sister, but I always wanted a brother. Darren had five brothers, and he's lost two of them. I can't replace what he's lost, but I want to do the best I can. It's an honor for me to have the opportunity to take care of Darren, to share my faith with him, to help him grow in his faith.

Having my family be a part of CrossFit Mayhem is satisfying. I've lost enough family to know how important family is, and my family needs to know that I care about them and that I love them. I don't want them to second-guess that. If something happens to me, I want them to know that I loved them.

CHAPTER 21

GET FIT

ONE OF THE HIGHLIGHTS of owning a CrossFit affiliate is being in the middle of the CrossFit community on a daily basis. To me, that sense of community is probably the biggest selling point I can make to people curious about starting CrossFit. I think it's the job of CrossFit affiliates to show people that our sport is largely about community and how supportive everyone is of each other.

I've been to CrossFit affiliates all around the world, and wherever I've gone, that sense of community has been there. It amazes me how little difference there can be between CrossFit Mayhem and CrossFit Seoul, for instance. The people look different and the languages aren't the same, but the equipment's the same, the gym feels the same, and in both places the people are helping each other through workouts, holding each other accountable, and hanging out together afterward. *Family* is almost a cliché in sports, but there really is a sense of family at all the affiliates I've visited.

We joke about there being a "shared suffering" for CrossFitters, but there is truth in that. The intensity of the workouts drives CrossFitters together. You develop a common bond because you understand what the person next to you is going through. You know what the other person is feeling.

Those on the outside who just look in can't begin to understand what CrossFit is truly all about. Sure, they can see that the workouts are difficult, although they don't know how difficult they really are. But more important, they don't realize just how tight the CrossFit community is until they become a part of it. CrossFit really isn't what they see on TV.

CrossFit isn't about the Games—it's about getting people fitter for life.

CrossFit isn't about me or Dan Bailey or any other athlete you want to name—it's about the sixty-year-old woman who started coming to our gym so she could pick up and play with her grandkid. It's about the middle-aged guy who wants to get back to the level of fitness he enjoyed in college. It's about the younger people who are already in pretty good shape and want to be able to lift more, be more flexible, and move faster than they can now. It's about the lady recovering from surgery and the twenty-year-old who's ecstatic because she just performed her first muscle-up. It's about the community.

When people join our gym, the first thing we will usually try to establish is their purpose for wanting to do CrossFit. The most common reasons we hear are to get fitter or to eliminate frustration over not being able to do a specific activity as well as desired or even at all.

If people don't have a purpose, we try to help them identify one, and we don't consider "to look better" a good purpose. Looking better is a by-product of doing CrossFit, but we encourage people to find more practical reasons for working out.

We want people to be more active in everyday life. That's one reason CrossFit emphasizes the kinds of movements we all perform every day—lifting, pulling, pushing, etc. That's the idea behind CrossFit's definition of health, which, according to CrossFit founder Greg Glassman, is "increased work capacity across broad time, modal, and age domains." What does that mean? Work capacity means the ability to perform physical tasks. Broad time, modal, and age domains means we want you to be able to perform those tasks no matter whether it's a short, intense task or a long one, no matter what kind of work is involved, and no matter how old you are. In other words, we want that grandmother to be able to pick up her grandkid, and that man to be able to play more golf without hurting, and those young athletes to be in better shape and improve their skills for their sports. Even the thought of delaying by a few years that move into the nursing home later in life is good motivation.

We don't try to weed out those who aren't real serious about coming to work out. We don't need to because CrossFit has a good way of doing that on its own. CrossFit is not a sport you do just to do it. It requires too much of you to continue doing it without an identifiable and practical purpose.

A person's motivation factor is crucial in CrossFit, and their successes can inspire an entire gym, including the coaches.

There is a doctor's wife who trains in our gym, and for two or three years she was afraid of handstand push-ups. She'd try, but her fear would prevent her from being able to do one. Then came the day when she finally did not just one but two in a row. She started jumping up and down, shouting and celebrating because it was about much more than a handstand push-up. She had overcome a fear that had been holding her back.

I've watched countless people who had zero confidence that they would be able to lift a certain weight. Then when they push it over their head for the first time, you would think *they* had won a CrossFit Games.

The muscle-up is a key benchmark, and every CrossFitter remembers the first time they accomplished it. I love being there when people get their first muscle-up. Muscle-ups on the rings are a core CrossFit movement, but they're tricky. Lots of people try for months or even years before they're able to do it. When they finally do get the hang of it, it's a great moment. They're up there on the rings with a great big smile on their face, and it's fun to see.

Dan has worked with a man who had ACL reconstruction surgery at age twelve and has had eight or nine more knee surgeries since. The man could do very little with his knees. But he started training with Dan, and after a few months of really busting his butt, he got to the point where he was doing full squats and other movements involving his knees as capably as any other person. It was impressive and inspiring to both Dan and me.

Witnessing those types of moments and being able to fully appreciate all that went into those accomplishments is rewarding. These are people who have a goal, but they don't know how to achieve it. We, as coaches, are able to give them the tools they need to make it happen.

It's funny to watch someone react by asking, "You mean I could have been doing this the whole time?"

Mental Training

CrossFit reveals so much about people.

For me, physically, I've learned that the sky is my limit. I've done so many things physically in CrossFit that I'd never thought possible. When I first started, for example, my max snatch weight was 165. In early 2013, I reached a big goal I'd had for several months when I snatched 300. A few years earlier, I never would have thought I'd even be setting 300 as a goal. Every day begins with the potential of learning something new about myself—that ability to say, "You mean I could have been doing this the whole time?"

The mental side is so important in CrossFit. Like I said earlier, I believe it accounts for 70 percent of what we do.

Everybody has a breaking point mentally. Certain workouts tend to push people to that point more frequently than others. As a coach, I've learned to recognize when someone is beginning to reach that point. I get curious to see whether that person will pick himself back up or allow his mind to break him. When the mind says, *No more*, he's reached that breaking point. He's done. There's no reason to push him to continue the workout.

I like to figure out the mental side of the people I work with to learn what makes them tick. Then I want to push their breaking points higher. The way to do that is to take them to a place they would not have known they could reach. The mind is almost like the muscles we develop. Muscles are made stronger by increasing their workloads. So is the mind. We grow stronger mentally by successfully tackling increased mental workloads.

I wish I could discover why people quit. I've often wondered if it's because of how they were raised. Among the college athletes I've worked with, I've seen too many who simply weren't mentally tough. They had all the natural gifts in the world, but they were lazy. They obviously had never been pushed by someone or by themselves. They had achieved success relying on their natural abilities until they made it to college, but all of a sudden they were surrounded by other athletes who had the same natural abilities as them, plus the mental toughness they didn't possess. The mentally weak ones didn't seem to have a purpose to work toward. They seemed to ask themselves, *Why should I put myself through this?* And nothing from their life experience could provide a good answer that would prevent them from quitting.

I've asked that question of myself. Especially after the 2010 Games, when I would think, *I don't want to do this. I don't care.* Or *I've got a few months before I really need to start doing this, so I don't have to put myself through this right now.* Those were the days when my upbringing bailed me out. I didn't know it when I was pulling nails out of boards for no apparent reason and hauling cinder blocks to the second barn and then back to the first one, but my parents were helping me develop mental toughness.

The mental brings the physical along. The body can handle more than we think. There are scientific explanations I have learned in my exercise science studies that I won't bore you with, but the more we give our bodies, the better our bodies will be. There's something called the Overload Principle, and it teaches that if we lift more weight, we get stronger, and if we do more reps, we increase endurance. It doesn't matter whether I'm working with athletes, kids, or adults—when they continuously give their bodies more and harder tasks, their bodies adapt.

The bodies God gave us truly are incredible. As Psalm 139:14 says, "I praise you, for I am fearfully and won-derfully made." God designed us so that when we want to stand upright, our bones and muscles work together to make it happen. Scientists can build robots, but they have yet to figure out how to build a robot that can move like a human. As I've learned about all the intricacies of the human body, I've been blown away by how God created us and put our bodies together.

How to Get Started

I consider myself blessed to be in a position where I can help people do more with the bodies that God gave them—to discover more of what they were created to be and do. With that in mind, I'd like to offer three short pieces of advice for those who are interested in starting CrossFit.

1. Join a CrossFit affiliate.

CrossFit affiliate memberships aren't free. I get that, and as a gym owner who has to pay the bills, I know why. It's true that although there is CrossFit-specific equipment, many of CrossFit's movements can be done without equipment and away from a gym. But still, in my opinion, the advantages of joining a CrossFit gym are worth the money.

First, coaches will be with you, teaching you proper techniques (for safety purposes), helping you become fluent in movements, guiding you through workouts, pushing you, and holding you accountable.

Second, you just can't get the benefits of a CrossFit community unless you're in one. The members of our gym range in age from preteens to a couple in their early sixties. That "shared suffering" I mentioned earlier erases differences between people while they're in the middle of a workout together. Being with other CrossFitters brings you encouragement and accountability.

Ask CrossFitters why they continue to put themselves through demanding workouts, and if the answers you receive are like the ones I've heard, it's the sense of accomplishment. Conquering a workout is an accomplishment, and accomplishments should be shared and celebrated with others.

If you need help finding a CrossFit gym (a lot of CrossFitters refer to their gyms as "boxes"), nothing is better than trusted friends' references. But outside of that, I recommend you visit a gym and look around to see if the coaches are actually with the people working out. If a class is kind of wandering around on its own and the coach isn't on the floor with them or is off to himself checking e-mails or texting, look for a different gym.

CrossFit's growth is leading to more and more affiliates, and that means more choices. Visit as many as you can, and be sure to take advantage of those that offer a free introductory workout.

2. Don't be intimidated.

Let's make something clear right off the bat: you are not going to start at the level of others who have already been doing CrossFit, and no one—not the coaches and not the other members—will expect you to. So don't put that expectation on yourself, either.

Feel better now?

Our gym offers introductory classes for new members. If they've done CrossFit before or have a higher level of fitness, they are able to test out fairly quickly and begin the more advanced workouts. If not, we start them with the very basics. We explain CrossFit thoroughly, and we carefully and slowly teach them the movements and the proper techniques.

A good CrossFit coach will start you where you are and then progressively take you to where you want to be. That means tailoring workouts to each individual if need be. It also means you need to know your purpose and your goals going in. That will allow you to push yourself, under the guidance of your coach. You won't be expected to do more than you can do, but I assure you that you will be challenged to do more than you think you can do.

3. Have fun.

This one might seem obvious, but it is vital. CrossFit is going to be stressful, but it should be a fun and beneficial stress. CrossFit should bring you relief from the stress of the other areas of your life. The biggest problem I see in CrossFitters is that they turn CrossFit into additional negative stress.

CrossFit is supposed to make you fitter. It's supposed to make you healthier. So don't get too stressed about it. Have fun with it. That doesn't mean that all the workouts will be fun, but you can almost always find a way to enjoy them.

One thing I've noticed about CrossFitters, regardless of their age or where in the world they work out, is that CrossFitters tend to be happy people.

CHAPTER 22

WHAT IT TAKES TO WIN

As I said in chapter 3, my life's top priorities can be described with three *F*s: faith, family, and fitness. Since the rope rerouted my life following the 2010 Games, I've made every effort to keep them in that order of importance.

I have to laugh when I'm asked how long I'll continue to compete in CrossFit. I mean, I'm only twenty-five and I'm being asked when I'll "retire"! I don't have a time frame in mind, but I suspect that the day I'm competing for fifth or sixth place will be when I start looking toward the next chapter in my life.

Winning the Games is great, but competing and the year-round training take their toll. The training after I reach

"Go Time" and the travel I do take me away from Hillary, and we do intend to start a family. When we have kids, I won't neglect them or fail to spend enough time with them. Both of my parents were there for me when I was growing up—and they still are—and I'm going to do the same for my kids.

I accept that a time will come when I'm no longer a contender to be standing on the medal podium at the end of the Games. There will be a point at which my body will no longer be able to produce at the highest level. Other athletes will come along who are younger and stronger. Everyone has an age at which their performance begins to fall off. I don't know what age that will be for me, and I don't spend time thinking about it. When it's gone, it's gone. Frankly I don't worry about it because it's not something I can control. All I can control is trying to be out there competing for championships for as long as I am able.

I do hope that my career won't end as the result of injury because I don't want to be forced out of competition. I want to give it all I can for as long as I can and then walk away. I'd prefer to decide when that time comes, not have the decision made for me.

As a competitor, the moment I have to step away from competing is not one I look forward to, but I can accept it before it happens because fitness is third on my list of priorities. It wasn't that way just a few short years ago, but now there are more important priorities in my life than being a CrossFit athlete.

That's a direct reflection of no longer finding my identity

through CrossFit. During this season of my life, I believe God has chosen CrossFit to be the avenue through which I can best glorify Him. I'm doing what God has called me to do, obediently using the physical and mental abilities He has blessed me with.

Since I'm into fitness, one Bible verse that stands out to me when I read it is 1 Corinthians 6:19-20: "Do you not know that your body is a temple of the Holy Spirit within you, whom you have from God? You are not your own, for you were bought with a price. So glorify God in your body."

The apostle Paul was instructing the Corinthian church to avoid sexual immorality because a sin against the body is a sin against the temple of the Holy Spirit. What's more, in verse 15, he wrote, "Do you not know that your bodies are members of Christ?" Jesus Christ paid the ultimate price by giving up His life on the cross. Paul called out those who were guilty of neglecting Christ's sacrifice by using their bodies for their own sinful pleasures instead of for glorifying God.

When I study those verses, I view them from an athlete's perspective. I believe God gave me my body for a purpose and that I'd better make the most of what I've been given and use it for His glory, not mine. I realize that to others I have become one of the guys on the videos like those I watched when I started CrossFit in the barn. But I don't see myself as being someone to look up to like I did Jason Khalipa and Chris Spealler and Mikko Salo. I really don't. I mean, all I do is work out. I'm just like all the other CrossFitters in a gym who'll never be on television. I work out just like they do.

At the same time, I recognize that I am in the spotlight more now. I'm interviewed more, and that puts me in a position to be able to inspire people. But I don't want to inspire them only physically and mentally. I want to inspire them spiritually, too. I hope that the more people learn about me as an athlete, the more they will want to learn about me as a Christian.

I've received criticism for sharing my faith publicly as much as I do, but I've received much more affirmation. I've been given this platform through CrossFit and my sponsors, and I've tried to achieve a balance. I don't want to be too preachy and turn people off, yet I also am committed to fulfilling the responsibility I have as a Christian to share the drastic difference following Jesus has made in my life. Honestly I don't know if I've found that balance or not.

There have been people who have told me, "What you've done is great because you've got me thinking about why I do what I do."

On the other hand, others have told me, "You don't do enough with what you've got. You're not out there quoting the Bible enough and telling people they need Jesus."

It's tough, and with social media it's extremely easy for people to be critical. On Twitter, with the number of followers I have, I know it's impossible to post a tweet without upsetting someone somewhere. I know I've been ripped on Internet message boards for publicly demonstrating my Christianity.

I remember back to early 2011 when the change in my

life took place. I knew opportunities would come to share my faith publicly, and I thought ahead to the first time I would have a chance to do so in an interview. I was concerned about what the reaction would be. I didn't want to sound like an idiot. I was relatively new with my study of Scripture. I realized I had opportunities coming to say things that would cause people to think about issues they hadn't previously thought about, and I didn't want to mess up those opportunities. I wanted to avoid sounding like such a moron that people wouldn't become curious or go try to learn more about what it means to be a Christian.

Before one of those first interviews—I can't recall which one it was—I was thinking to myself, *Do I want to do this? What if I sound stupid to people who are Christians? What if I sound stupid to people who* aren't *Christians?* But I wasn't going to allow those thoughts to stop me from sharing my faith. *All right,* I told myself, *this is why I do what I do, so why not tell people about it?*

My confidence in publicly talking about the gospel increased the more I studied Scripture and read books about the Bible and Christianity. I've prayed that God would give me the strength and the courage to stand up for Him, and I've asked for wisdom so that I wouldn't sound like an idiot. Those were different prayers from when I was in high school and college. Back then, I was telling God what I wanted from Him. Now, I'm asking God for the help I need to do what He wants me to do for Him.

The reactions I get when I share my faith are not

something I'm overly concerned about anymore. I can do my best with the wisdom that God has given me to make a good presentation for Him, but I can do nothing about how people choose to respond. I'm not concerned about being rejected. Ultimately, the reason I do what I do is to please God. I can tell you with complete certainty that it is much easier to please God than it is to please people.

In the Sermon on the Mount, Jesus said, "Blessed are those who are persecuted for righteousness' sake, for theirs is the kingdom of heaven" (Matthew 5:10). I don't feel like I'm being persecuted for being a Christian, but that verse gives me a little extra drive when I'm criticized for sharing my faith. It gives me a bring-it-on attitude.

I'm not combative with my faith, but I'm also not afraid to share my beliefs and to explain the changes that have taken place within my heart over the past two and a half years.

Freed!

I try to grow in some way spiritually every day.

Just as CrossFit is about community, community is one of the most important things the church was formed to be. Just as members of the CrossFit community see one of their purposes as helping make other members more fit, it's the same with a spiritual community in helping make other members more spiritually fit.

In addition to the church that Hillary and I attend with Dan Bailey, I have a great faith support group around me that includes some of the people I've mentioned in this book like Chip Pugh, Donovan Degrie, and Thomas Cox. Doc Phillips—my former professor who, along with his wife, Amanda, was one of our first gym clients—has been influential in my continued spiritual growth and in helping me develop my Bible study habits. And of course Dan is always around to encourage me and challenge me.

Thomas still is one of my regular workout partners at CrossFit Mayhem. There are also some Tennessee Tech students I work out with who are a part of my faith support group. They belong to the University Christian Student Center, and although I'm not much older than they are, there are ways that I can help them in fitness and faith, and at the same time they can also help me strengthen my faith.

I have a couple of friends who have created an accountability system where if they don't read their Bible one day, they do thirty extra burpees. Granted, that could easily become a read-the-Bible-as-duty accountability system, but they're intentional about preventing that by keeping it fun, and it works for them.

Those are the friends who help keep me grounded.

Hillary is a huge influence in my spiritual life as well. She doesn't get caught up in all that "Rich Froning the CrossFitter" talk. She has a loving way of reminding me of who I really am and what my true priorities are when I come home feeling great about something I did at the gym, and I'm thankful she's that way.

Thomas is good about holding me accountable personally

and spiritually. "Are you reading your Bible?" he'll ask. "Are you tithing? Are you praying like you should?" Thomas helps hold me accountable not only by asking questions like those but also because I know that he's going to ask them—and I want to be able to answer yes.

Thomas once called me when I was on a trip and said, "Yeah, I'd like to talk to Rich. Not Rich Froning the CrossFit athlete. But Rich."

"All right, I get you," I told him.

Just because I'm a Christian doesn't mean I don't have to battle with pride. There has been only one perfect person who's walked this earth. I know I'm not perfect, and I know I can't be. I make mistakes, and I have weaknesses in my life that I need to work on. It's a steady battle.

It's just like fitness. I'm constantly testing myself in training to see what areas I need to work on. In life, tests come my way, and they show the areas where I'm weak and need to be strengthened, by God's grace and with His help.

I feel fortunate to have family and friends like Thomas, who, although he was being funny with me on the phone, had a serious message behind his joking.

That's what true friends—the people who really care for you—need to possess the courage to do.

My spiritual life has already changed for the better since I started competing in CrossFit, and I have no intention of it changing back. I know I have family and friends around me who feel the same way and are bold enough to say to me what needs to be said.

After all, they were my family and friends before I began CrossFit, and they're going to be my family and friends long after I'm through competing. All the people who know me as Rich the CrossFitter are going to forget about me one day. I won't compete forever, and there will be athletes who come along and make people forget whatever accomplishments I wind up with.

That is why I don't want to miss this present opportunity I've been given to introduce people to who I really am and to the reason why I am who I am.

People want to know what has enabled me to win back-to-back Games. The answer is simple: my faith. There is no doubt in my mind about that. So while people tell me that if not for the rope in 2010, I'd be a three-time Games winner, I'm convinced I wouldn't be.

If I had won the Games in 2010, I don't believe I would have won again. The way I think it would have played out is that, despite my lack of desire to compete in the months after those Games, I still would have returned to the Games, but I don't think I would have performed well at all.

In another place in the book of Matthew, Jesus told the parable of the laborers who were hired to work in the vineyard and how those who had been hired first became upset when those hired last received the same pay. In chapter 20, verse 16, Jesus spoke these well-known words: "So the last will be first, and the first last."

It is not lost on me that I became first at the Games only after I put God first in my life.

To be clear, I'm not saying that when I started developing a closer relationship with God, I prayed to win the Games and He decided to answer my prayer as a reward. Not at all. I wasn't praying to win. I was praying that I would glorify God regardless of where I finished.

The role that my deepening faith played in CrossFit is that it freed me. Before Chip and Donovan asked me the questions that started me on a new path in my spiritual journey, I was bound by all the pressure I was feeling.

There is a pressure that some athletes can thrive under, but then there is a pressure that restricts athletes' ability to perform. When I look back and evaluate the rope climb in 2010, I cracked under that second type of pressure. I was in first place going into the final workout. The championship was within my grasp just like the rope was. But I was caught unprepared.

I believe there is a parallel between life and CrossFit about always being prepared. I've experienced through my family how suddenly and unexpectedly a life can end. The lessons I've learned have impacted my thinking about what I would want my legacy to be. The truth is, while God knows what is ahead for all of us, we don't. We have to stay prepared, whether it be to answer a question regarding our faith or deal with a curveball that life throws us.

As an athlete, it's not easy for me to admit that I cracked under the pressure in my first Games. But I was a different person then. I changed early in 2011. I became a freed person. And I'm not talking about just as an athlete who could be nervous on a bus ride to the first event at Santa Monica Pier, call up the Bible on my phone, and experience a calming presence like I had never felt before. That wouldn't have been a life change; that would have been a sports change.

My life changed when, for what I consider the first time, I committed myself wholly to Christ. I learned to trust Him—to not sweat the small stuff and to stop becoming easily overwhelmed. I controlled my temper better because I stopped allowing things to get to me as quickly as they had before. I found peace in knowing that, as Jeremiah 29:11-13 says, God has a plan for my life. Because of that, the pressure was off of me to plot out all the details of my future.

I found my purpose in living to glorify God, not in competing to bring glory to myself. I found my identity not in a sport where I was one injury or one superior athlete away from people forgetting who I was, but in Christ, who gave His life for me so that I could spend eternity with Him.

Discovering my purpose didn't make me a better, stronger, and faster athlete, but it did free me to be a better, stronger, and faster athlete—the athlete God has created me to be.

And that is what it took for me to win.

After the Rope

In the main workout area at CrossFit Mayhem in Cookeville, there are climbing ropes hanging from the ceiling. Across the gym is a blue wall with *Galatians 6:14* painted in white letters, in the same font and design as my tattoo.

Adding the ropes was my idea. Painting the Bible reference was thought up by one of the ladies handling our interior decorating with Hillary. I returned from a trip to Chile, and there it was on the wall. I liked it immediately.

There is symbolism in the ropes and the verse being together in one place, because one led me to the other. The rope represents what I once was most known for; the verse represents what I most want to be known for.

It was a rope that exposed two of my weaknesses. One was obvious to CrossFit fans around the world. The other, more important one was visible only to me within my own heart.

The first weakness was corrected by learning how to hold on properly; the second was corrected by learning how to let go. As I began to dig deeper into the Bible, I let go of my pride and found my purpose in God.

The rope defined me until God's Word refined me. And what God's Word has taught me is that the key to truly winning is not to be first.

The key to winning is to put God first.

ACKNOWLEDGMENTS

FIRST, THANK YOU TO my Lord and Savior, Jesus Christ. This would never have happened without His guidance, His love, and His grace.

I'd like to thank my amazing wife, Hillary, for putting up with me while I am around. Thank you also for being so graceful and supportive of me no matter how well I do or don't do.

Thank you to Mom and Dad ("the original Rich Froning") for making me the man I am today.

Thank you to Kayla Beckham and Patty and Ali Masters for your undying support.

Thank you to Papa and Violet for being amazing grandparents.

Thank you to Darren for always being there, suffering through most workouts alongside me, and always trying to make me get one more rep.

Thank you to the way-too-many-to-list members of the Finn and Froning sides of my family.

Thank you to Donovan, Thomas, Chip, Mike Phillips, and Bret Ellis for aiding in my continual spiritual growth.

Thank you to Butch Chaffin for making me realize there is no substitute for hard work.

Thank you to Yvette Clark and Web Smith, my team, for allowing me to focus on competition amid all of the business.

Thank you to Charles and Tyler Peek, Justin Morgan, and Amanda Phillips for always being there at the Games to support me.

Thank you to the Cookeville Fire Department for the life lessons I learned while being on the job.

And a big thank you to CrossFit Inc. and its leaders—Greg Glassman, Dave Castro, and the rest—for allowing me the opportunity to excel in this great sport and in this great community. That means you, CrossFit Mayhem!

God bless, and thank you for reading.

COMMON CROSSFIT TERMS

THIS LIST OF common terms is not in any way complete, but it's a starting point for reference if you come across an unfamiliar term in this book or in CrossFit literature. Full definitions and video demonstrations of most of these terms can be found at various websites, including CrossFit.com.

Air Squat: a squat performed with no additional weight
Affiliate: an official CrossFit gym
Back Extension: an exercise performed by lowering the upper body from a position parallel to the ground to a position perpendicular to the ground, then raising it back up
Back Squat: a squat performed with a weighted barbell held on the shoulders behind the neck
Box: a common term used for a CrossFit gym
Box-Jump: jumping from the floor onto a box or raised platform

Bumper Plate: weightlifting plate designed to be dropped from overhead without damage

Burpee: explosive push-up with a jump at the end

Butterfly Kip: a kipping movement where the body moves in a continuous circular motion with no swinging or pausing at the top or bottom of the movement

Butterfly Pull-Up: a pull-up performed using a butterfly kip

Chest-to-Bar Pull-Up: a pull-up where the chest hits the bar

Clean: a weightlifting movement where a barbell is lifted from the floor to rack position at shoulder height

Clean-and-Jerk: a clean followed by a jerk (moving the bar to a locked-out position overhead)

Deadlift: lifting a barbell from the floor to waist height

Death by . . . : doing one rep of a given exercise the first minute, two reps the second minute, three reps the third minute, and so on, until you can't complete the proper number of reps within the minute allowed

Dip: lowering your body between parallel bars or gymnastic rings till the elbows are bent beyond 90 degrees, then pushing back up

Double-Under: jumping rope where the rope must pass two times under the feet on each jump

Farmer's Carry: carrying heavy objects in each hand over distance

For Time: a term indicating that a workout is timed

Front Squat: a squat performed while holding a barbell in rack position in front of the shoulders

GHD Sit-Up: a sit-up performed on a glute-ham developer

Ground-to-Overhead: lifting a barbell from the ground to an overhead position by any means necessary

Hand-Release Push-Up: push-up where the hands must come off the ground while the chest rests on the ground at the bottom of the movement

Handstand Push-Up: lowering the body from a handstand position to where the top of the head makes contact with the ground, then pushing back up

Handstand Walk: walking on your hands for distance while in a handstand position

Hang Clean: a clean starting with the barbell hanging at waist height (instead of on the ground)

Hip Extension: a back extension performed while maintaining the lumbar arch

Jerk: moving a barbell from shoulder height to overhead while dropping beneath the bar to catch it in a fully locked-out position

Kettlebell: a special rounded weight with a handle

Kettlebell Clean: a one-armed clean performed with a kettlebell

Kettlebell Snatch: a one-armed snatch performed with a kettlebell

Kettlebell Swing: a two-handed swing of a kettlebell from between the legs to overhead

Knees-to-Elbows: raising the lower body while hanging from a pull-up bar so that the knees make contact with the elbows

Kipping: moving the legs and body to use momentum to assist with a movement (such as pull-ups)

Muscle-Up: raising the body from a hanging position below an object (often gymnastic rings) to a locked-out position above the object

Olympic Lifts: snatch, clean, clean-and-jerk

Overhead Squat: a squat performed while holding a barbell overhead

Paleo: reference to the Paleo Diet, a diet advocated by Dr. Loren Cordain and utilized by many CrossFitters

Pistol: one-legged squat

Pood: used to describe kettlebell weights; one pood is roughly equivalent to 35 pounds

Power Clean: a clean performed with the bar starting on the ground—the bar is caught in an upright position, not a squat

Pull-Up: raising the body from a hanging position below a bar to a position where the chin is above the bar

Push-Jerk: a cross between a push-press and a true jerk

Push-Press: moving a bar from shoulder height to overhead by utilizing legs and triceps

Rack Position: holding a bar at shoulder height in front of the shoulders with wrists bent and elbows forward

Ring Dip: a dip performed on gymnastic rings

Row: rowing done on a machine (often a Concept2 rower)

Shoulder Press: lifting a bar from shoulder height to overhead using only the triceps, no legs

Snatch: lifting a weight from the ground to overhead in one smooth movement, not stopping at rack position

Split Jerk: a jerk performed by catching the bar overhead in a locked-out position with one foot forward and one back

Split Snatch: executing a snatch with one foot forward and one back, then bringing your feet together while holding the bar in a locked-out position

Squat: squatting with feet flat on the floor until the crease of the hip dips below the knee, then standing back up

Squat Clean: lifting a barbell from the ground to shoulder height and catching it in a full squat position, then standing back up

Strict Pull-Up: a pull-up performed with no kipping

Sumo Deadlift High-Pull: lifting a barbell (or kettlebell) from the ground to right under the chin, with feet just over shoulder-width apart and hands gripping the bar inside the feet

Tabata: 20 seconds of work, 10 seconds of rest,
8 rounds per exercise

Thruster: a front squat followed immediately by an
overhead press

Toes-to-Bar: hanging from a pull-up bar and bringing
the lower body up until the toes make contact with
the bar

Wall-Ball: medicine ball that is thrown against a target
on a wall; each throw starts with a full squat

Workout of the Day: Every day most affiliates (as well
as CrossFit.com) post a workout that all athletes
who belong to that affiliate will perform; also called
a WOD.

COMMON CROSSFIT
ABBREVIATIONS

AMRAP: As many rounds (or reps) as possible
BB: Barbell
C2B: Chest-to-Bar Pull-Up
DB: Dumbbell
DL: Deadlift
D/U: Double-Under
EMOTM: Every minute on the minute
FGB: Fight Gone Bad
GHD: Glute-Ham Developer
HRPU: Hand-Release Push-Up
HSPU: Handstand Push-Up
KB: Kettlebell
KBS: Kettlebell Swing
KTE: Knees-to-Elbows
MB: Medicine Ball
MOD: Workout modified
MBSC: Medicine Ball Squat Clean
M/U: Muscle-Up

OHS: Overhead Squat
PU: Pull-Up
RM: Repetition maximum, or rep max (in pounds)
RX: Workout performed as prescribed
SDHP: Sumo Deadlift High-Pull
T2B: Toes-to-Bar
TGU: Turkish Get-Up
WOD: Workout of the Day

CLASSIC CROSSFIT
WORKOUTS

THESE WORKOUTS SERVE as benchmarks for people to compare their performance against others. More important, they are benchmarks you can use to compare your own performance against your previous efforts and measure improvement. The best-known workouts have women's names—like hurricanes, which is appropriate given how you feel after one of them. All workouts are performed for time unless otherwise indicated.

Annie: 50-40-30-20-10 of double-unders and sit-ups
Angie: 100 pull-ups, 100 push-ups, 100 sit-ups, 100 squats
Barbara: 5 rounds of 20 pull-ups, 30 push-ups, 40 sit-ups, 50 squats; rest 3 minutes between rounds
Chelsea: 30 rounds of 5 pull-ups, 10 push-ups, 15 squats, every minute on the minute
Cindy: AMRAP in 20 minutes of 5 pull-ups, 10 push-ups, 15 squats

CrossFit Total: Sum of single-rep max (for pounds) of back squat, shoulder press, deadlift

Diane: 21-15-9 of deadlifts (225 lbs) and handstand push-ups

Elizabeth: 21-15-9 of cleans (135 lbs) and ring dips

Eva: 5 rounds of an 800-meter run, 30 kettlebell swings (2 pood or 70 lbs), 30 pull-ups

Fight Gone Bad: 3 rounds of max reps in one minute each of wall-ball shots (20 lbs), sumo deadlift high-pulls (75 lbs), box-jumps (24 inches), push-presses (75 lbs), and row (calories, not reps); rest one minute between rounds

Filthy Fifty: 50 reps of box-jumps (24 inches), jumping pull-ups, walking lunge steps, push-presses (45 lbs), kettlebell swings (1 pood or 35 lbs), back extensions, wall-ball shots (20 lbs), knees-to-elbows, burpees, double-unders

Fran: 21-15-9 of thrusters (95 lbs) and pull-ups

Grace: 30 clean-and-jerks (135 lbs)

Helen: 3 rounds of a 400-meter run, 21 kettlebell swings (1.5 pood or 55 lbs), 12 pull-ups

Isabel: 30 snatches (135 lbs)

Karen: 150 wall-ball shots (20 lbs)

Kelly: 5 rounds of a 400-meter run, 30 box-jumps (24 inches), 30 wall-ball shots (20 lbs)

Mary: AMRAP in 20 minutes of 5 handstand push-ups, 10 pistols, 15 pull-ups

Nancy: 5 rounds of a 400-meter run, 15 overhead squats (95 lbs)

Nasty Girls: 3 rounds of 50 squats, 7 muscle-ups, 10 hang cleans (135 lbs)

Nicole: AMRAP in 20 minutes of a 400-meter run, max pull-ups

Tabata Something Else: 8 Tabata rounds (20 seconds of work, 10 seconds of rest) each of pull-ups, push-ups, sit-ups, squats

CROSSFIT HERO WORKOUTS

CROSSFIT PERIODICALLY prescribes workouts that are named in honor of soldiers, police officers, or firefighters who have died in the line of duty. Hero workouts are designed to be particularly difficult; by performing these workouts, athletes honor the memory of the fallen hero. This is by no means an exhaustive list, but it includes some of the better-known hero workouts. All workouts are performed for time unless otherwise indicated.

Badger (in honor of Navy Chief Petty Officer Mark Carter, who was killed in Iraq on December 11, 2007): 3 rounds of 30 squat cleans (95 lbs), 30 pull-ups, 800-meter run

Blake (in honor of Navy Chief Cryptologic Technician David Blake McLendon, who was killed in Afghanistan on September 21, 2010): 4 rounds of 100-foot walking lunge steps with 45-lb plate held

overhead, 30 box-jumps (24 inches), 20 wall-ball
shots (20 lbs), 10 handstand push-ups

Bradshaw (in honor of Army First Lieutenant Brian
Bradshaw, who was killed in Afghanistan on June 25,
2009): 10 rounds of 3 handstand push-ups, 6 deadlifts
(225 lbs), 12 pull-ups, 24 double-unders

Collin (in honor of Navy Special Warfare Operator
Chief Collin Thomas, who was killed in Afghanistan
on August 18, 2010): 6 rounds of a 400-meter
sandbag carry (50 lbs), 12 push-presses (115 lbs),
12 box-jumps (24 inches), 12 sumo deadlift
high-pulls (95 lbs)

Daniel (in honor of Army Sergeant First Class Daniel
Crabtree, who was killed in Iraq on June 8, 2006):
50 pull-ups, 400-meter run, 21 thrusters (95 lbs),
800-meter run, 21 thrusters (95 lbs), 400-meter run,
50 pull-ups

Danny (in honor of Oakland SWAT Sergeant Daniel
Sakai, who was killed in the line of duty on March 21,
2009): AMRAP in 20 minutes of 30 box-jumps
(24 inches), 20 push-presses (115 lbs), 30 pull-ups

DT (in honor of USAF Staff Sergeant Timothy Davis,
who was killed in Afghanistan on February 20,
2009): 5 rounds of 12 deadlifts, 9 hang cleans,
6 push-jerks (all at 155 lbs)

Jack (in honor of Army Staff Sergeant Jack Martin III,
who was killed in the Philippines on September 29,
2009): AMRAP in 20 minutes of 10 push-presses

(115 lbs), 10 kettlebell swings (1.5 pood or 55 lbs),
10 box-jumps (24 inches)

Josh (in honor of Army Staff Sergeant Joshua Hager,
who was killed in Iraq on February 22, 2007):
21 overhead squats (95 lbs), 42 pull-ups, 15 overhead
squats, 30 pull-ups, 9 overhead squats, 18 pull-ups

Manion (in honor of Marine Corps First Lieutenant
Travis Manion, who was killed in Iraq on April 29,
2007): 7 rounds of a 400-meter run and 29 back
squats (135 lbs)

Michael (in honor of Navy Lieutenant Michael
McGreevy, who was killed in Afghanistan on
June 28, 2005): 3 rounds of an 800-meter run,
50 back extensions, 50 sit-ups

Murph (in honor of Navy Lieutenant Michael Murphy,
who was killed in Afghanistan on June 28, 2005):
one-mile run, 100 pull-ups, 200 push-ups,
300 squats, one-mile run; 20-lb vest optional

Nate (in honor of Navy Chief Petty Officer Nate Hardy,
who was killed in Iraq on February 4, 2008): AMRAP
in 20 minutes of 2 muscle-ups, 4 handstand push-ups,
8 kettlebell swings (2 pood or 70 lbs)

Randy (in honor of Randy Simmons, LAPD, who
was killed in the line of duty on February 6, 2008):
75 snatches (75 lbs)

RJ (in honor of LAPD Officer and Marine Corps
reservist Sergeant Major Robert Cottle, who was
killed in Afghanistan on March 24, 2010): 5 rounds

of an 800-meter run, 5 rope climbs (15 feet),
50 push-ups

Roy (in honor of Marine Corps Sergeant Michael Roy,
who was killed in Afghanistan on July 8, 2009):
5 rounds of 15 deadlifts (225 lbs), 20 box-jumps
(24 inches), 25 pull-ups

INDEX OF NAMES